PRESSU

RE G⛳LF

OVERCOMING
CHOKING AND
FRUSTRATION

MICHAEL CLARKSON

RAINCOAST BOOKS
Vancouver

Raincoast Books gratefully acknowledges the ongoing support of the Canada Council for the Arts; the British Columbia Arts Council; and the Government of Canada through the Department of Canadian Heritage Book Publishing Industry Development Program (BPIDP).

Typeset by Ingrid Paulson

National Library of Canada Cataloguing in Publication Data

Clarkson, Michael, 1948–
  Pressure golf: overcoming choking and frustration

  Includes bibliographical references and index.
  ISBN 1-55192-605-9

  1. Golf—Psychological aspects. I. Title.
GV979.P75C52 2003   796.352'01'9   C2002-911414-4

Library of Congress Catalogue Number: 2002096042

Raincoast Books   *In the United States:*
9050 Shaughnessy Street   Publishers Group West
Vancouver, British Columbia   1700 Fourth Street
Canada   Berkeley, California
www.raincoast.com   USA   94710

At Raincoast Books we are committed to protecting the environment and to the responsible use of natural resources. We are acting on this commitment by working with suppliers and printers to phase out our use of paper produced from ancient forests. This book is one step towards that goal. It is printed on 100% ancient-forest-free paper (100% post-consumer recycled), processed chlorine and acid free, and supplied by New Leaf Paper. It is printed with vegetable-based inks by Friesens. For further information, visit our website at www.raincoast.com. We are working with Markets Initiative (www.oldgrowthfree.com) on this project.

Printed and bound in Canada.

10 9 8 7 6 5 4 3 2 1

To Tony Vanderklei and golfers like him,
who take the game seriously,
but only when it's called for.

"The tension makes you grip the club too tight … it was like somebody standing very close to you, crossing into your personal space. I felt like the roof was falling down on me."

— Lorie Kane, describing the pressure of playing before her home Canadian fans in the 1999 du Maurier Classic in Calgary

"The players don't like to talk about [choking]. What you saw there was U.S. Open nerves big time. Goosen would make that putt 500 times in a row. It should have been the easiest two-putt I've ever seen, uphill and easy. Players often say afterward they misread these putts, but it's often a fib. It's nerves. There are a lot of lessons to be learned from this."

—TV *commentator Johnny Miller on Retief Goosen's shocking three-putt from 12 feet to send the 2001 U.S. Open into a playoff*

TABLE OF CONTENTS

INTRODUCTION

"Golfers need to understand more about why they choke ... I get nervous before every shot. It's how you deal with it that determines whether you will be a success."

— Tiger Woods to the author

Why do we need another book about the mental side of golf? As Tiger Woods says, we need to keep exploring the important subject of why golfers choke, an area that still holds many mysteries. Until now, it has not been investigated in a serious manner. For one thing, if golf is supposed to be such a relaxing escape, why do golfers so often get tense?

Choking continues to inhibit improvement, achievement and enjoyment of the game at all levels. Here's an example: over the course of their careers, few top touring pros have a better Sunday scoring average than their average during the first three days of a tournament. Not even the greatest of the greats — Jack Nicklaus, Tiger Woods or Annika Sorenstam — generally perform better under pressure. (Of course, Sunday scoring is a complex issue involving pin placements, but many players admit that final-round pressure is what gets to them more often than not.)

"A lot of times, you don't actually win so much; it's a case of all the other guys lose," says Nicklaus, winner of an unprecedented 18 major PGA Championships.

If the pros can't succeed consistently under pressure with all their advantages of golf science, coaching and psychology, what effect does pressure have on the high handicappers? In almost every area, golf has improved in recent years — in the quality of the courses and equipment, swing techniques, teaching and in the volume of world-class players, and yet the United States Golf Association reports that scores among amateurs have not gone down. Our ability to deal with pressure in competitive golf has not kept pace. As well, many psychologists report more pressure in our society than ever before, including the high stress levels we all feel at home, work and play.

This book is one of the first specific looks at "choking," a phenomenon that seriously affects every golfer today, hacker or scratch player, young or old. The *emotional* side of golf has not been adequately explored; the causes and effects of pressure haven't been studied properly.

How many of us are aware that we have a potent and unwieldy *fear defence system* that reacts with powerful hormones, such as adrenaline, to each little worry and potential threat we feel on the golf course?

My definition of choking is: *failure experienced by athletes under pressure when emotions, particularly fear, negatively interfere with their normal technique, their focus or their decision-making.* We see this when a baseball batter tenses up and strikes out in the bottom of the ninth, when a basketball player freezes at the foul line and when a field-goal kicker uncharacteristically hooks the ball wide in the dying seconds of a football game. In golf, choking often occurs when someone worries about the importance of a shot, resulting in muscles tensing up, which causes problems in the swing.

Sometimes instructors oversimplify this complex subject by telling golfers to just think positively and take a couple of deep breaths, and the nerves will calm. Of course, this can have short-term benefits, but many golfers need to stay calm for the long haul. Part of the problem is that, until now, we have focused heavily on treating the *symptoms* of choking rather than the *causes*, which include attitudes, beliefs, values and ego issues. *Why we choke* is a more important question to answer, so the symptoms don't keep popping up. If you are serious about addressing the mental and emotional issues — and we all have them to some degree — it may take a little patience and work. But consider the investment you are making in your golf game. A little extra effort will reduce frustration and lower your scores and ultimately increase your enjoyment of the game, whether you are a once-a-week duffer or a highly competitive player.

My research suggests there is hope. A journalist since 1967, I have been researching fear management and how to perform better in pressure situations since 1988. More recently, I have turned my attention to emotions in golf. Readers of my stories in the *Toronto Star*, on golf.com and of my first two books, *Competitive Fire* and *Intelligent Fear*, have reported that my recommendations have helped their golf games.

Many of the issues in this book have been discussed elsewhere by such progressive golf analysts as Bob Rotella, Patrick J. Cohn and W. Timothy Gallwey. And yet, despite all the golf books, magazine articles, TV shows and websites out there, despite all the sports psychologists, golfers don't seem to be winning the battle against choking, or at least the progress is slow.

I have chosen to focus on *fear* as one of the major reasons why golfers choke under pressure, particularly our fear we have of what other people think of our game. Such worry can blow one shot way out of proportion. Fear is the number one distraction, the chief cause of tension on the golf course. Without it, there is no physical arousal of the *fear defence system*. There is fear of failing; fear of succeeding and having to live up to higher expectations; fear of loss of control; fear of loss of earnings (for professionals); fear of the fear reaction itself and fear of criticism. When we start seeing stress for what it is — a natural fear response — we can make it more manageable. It should be pointed out, though, that fear and controlled anger have produced some of the greatest performances of all time from golfers who have occasionally been highly motivated to stick it to their critics — Nicklaus in the 1986 Masters, Karrie Webb in winning her first major in 1999 and Woods as he dominates the PGA in the early years of the 21st century. The use of controlled emotions, especially *intelligent fear*, is also behind some of the in-the-zone experiences golfers report occasionally.

Some of my opinions may be unpleasant to read at first. Who among us likes to be accused of being afraid or insecure? Who wants to hear that a possible cause of our choking has to do with our ego? And yet we must become consciously aware of ourselves and our potential hidden motives if we are to reduce frustration and add to our enjoyment of what can be a marvellous game. Additionally, we must become more consciously aware of our physical reaction when our fear defence system kicks in, as it does dozens of times a day, on and off the golf course.

Some of the viewpoints I present in the book are opinions, but most of the theories, conclusions and speculations have been carefully made after interviews with clinical professionals and golf experts. I am not a certified psychologist, but after more than three decades as a journalist, fear researcher, amateur sports coach and athlete, I have come to learn what works in the face of pressure and fear, and how to get into a zone of heightened awareness.

The quotes in this book come from a wide variety of sources, including about 500 interviews I've conducted with professional and amateur golfers, instructors and psychologists; newspapers and magazines such as *Golf Magazine*, *Golf Digest* and *Sports Illustrated*; and books such as *Golf Is Not a Game of Perfect* and *The Inner Game of Golf*. Many of these are listed at the end of this book.

Plan of Action

Sounds pretty grave, doesn't it, all this talk about fear? But fear is with us every day of our lives. It is the basis of both our daily distress and our remarkable accomplishments. Psychologists say that too much fear can kill us, and yet without it we cannot survive. It is the most powerful resource we possess, allowing us to survive little and large crises at home, at work and on the golf course.

Sadly, fear's legacy in golf is most often a negative one. In a difficult game loaded with distractions, fear is the worst distraction of all. It keeps high handicappers from improving, prevents non-duffers from taking up the wonderful sport and even has a detrimental effect on the seasoned pros.

The hard truth is that our human behaviour and our mind-body emotional system are not a natural match for anybody's golf game. When we get nervous, we react physically the same way we did millions of years ago, only now we have exchanged a big-headed club for one with a titanium shaft. And so we must train our emotional reactions, our fear defence system.

It can be done. It *has* been done — too infrequently, yes — by every one of us from time to time. Too often, we rely on quick fixes, as Rich Beem did to help him capture the 2002 PGA Championship. Before each round, he took a good swig of Pepto-Bismol to calm his nervous stomach. But we need a broader strategy so that our stomach does not keep acting up, so that our backswing does not keep getting tight. Through awareness and changing our techniques and ways of thinking, we can make adrenaline-fuelled achievements happen more often. We are in a confused time in our evolution. As we evolve, we must take the great things from nature and try to apply them to our sophisticated yet cluttered lives.

The strategy I have designed, with input from the great thinkers, teachers and players of the sport, is boiled down to just four basic strategies, each of which will be examined by a full section in this book:

1. **Awareness** — being fully aware of our mind and body's reaction to pressure, knowing it can trigger our arousal system to, at worst, disrupt our swing and focus, or, at best, to sharpen our resolve and our skills.
2. **Pressure management** — keeping pressure at manageable levels through practice, attitude, use of our resources and keeping the game in perspective.
3. **Focus** — trusting ourselves, becoming less self-conscious. This includes developing strong focus, a pre-shot routine and something constructive to do between shots.
4. **Managing emotional chemistry** — identifying our nervousness and changing our emotional chemistry, either by calming down or getting fired up, or by redirecting the feelings into our game.

The best model for this four-pronged plan is probably Tiger Woods. We think so much of his physical skills, but he is also ahead of the pack mentally and emotionally. He is aware of his feelings of arousal; he keeps his pressure at optimal levels through training; he largely plays to his own expectations; and he focuses through fear and even uses it from time to time. We can't necessarily equal Tiger and other pros in physical skills and in training opportunities, but perhaps we can in mental and emotional skills.

Although golfers are frightened of choking, they also seem fascinated by it. A fellow reporter at the *Toronto Star* told me he watches the televised PGA tournaments each Sunday "to see who will choke this time." And yet when Greg Norman collapsed in the 1996 Masters, he received thousands of letters sympathizing with him and applauding his handling of it. How well we handle such moments will determine how much success and fun we have on the golf course.

STRATEGY NO. 1:
AWARENESS

This section explores the psychology and the mechanics of why we some-times choke as golfers. It details how our defensive reactions can set off our nervous system and create havoc with our swing, or how it can actually help our game.

In Chapter 1 we see that worrying about what other golfers may think of us seems to be the number one cause of choking on the golf course. Chapter 2 deals with the primitive emergency fear system. In Chapter 3, we see that nowadays we set off this system by defending our ego rather than our physical bodies. This defensive response usually has a negative effect in the complex game of golf. In Chapters 4 and 5, we examine how over-arousal can negatively impact our swing and our overall golf game, but in Chapter 6, we see the "good side" of arousal and how successful players tap into its benefits. Chapter 7 looks at the different fear reactions among genders, ages and golfing situations.

"I don't know what the secret to golf is. I know part of my problem is I always over-try because I always have been told I have great talent. But I have never achieved my talent or achieved what a lot of people, my coaches, family and friends, think I could have. And it's because my brain always gets in the way."

— LPGA *player Patti Rizzo*

CHAPTER 1

WORRY:
Letting Other People Choke You

If you think your golf swing is unique, you should have seen Dr. David Cookson's. He would start the club face not from the ground, but from way up behind his head, then bring it down like a guillotine onto the ball. Cookson avoided the backswing because he was always nervous about his golf game. He *choked* so often, he developed what golfers call the "yips."

The yips is golf terminology for repeatedly choking over a shot, usually in reference to putting. It is viewed as a mental and emotional — and perhaps partly physical — disorder suffered on the greens and fairways of golf courses across the globe (some may call it an epidemic). Many golfers are squeamish even saying it: the yips.

For many years, Cookson had been a single-digit handicapper in Madison, Wisconsin, but increasingly he had been freezing over the ball, especially during pressure shots. "He could not make the club move," said Gene Haas, executive director of the Wisconsin State Golf Association. "He had to yell something like

'Geronimo!' that overrode something in his mind that was not allowing him to take the club back."

Physician, heal thyself. Dr. Cookson, who once finished tenth in the state's amateur championship, was so serious about getting his golf game back he went to a psychologist who used hypnotism to help people deal with phobias and other psychological issues. During one session, it was revealed that Cookson had tried all his life to please his mother, who demanded perfection. "[The hypnotist] said that whenever I practised, I should imagine the ball was my mother's head," Cookson told me. "I never quite did that. But I never froze over the ball again. Freud said that if you understood the reason for your phobia, it will disappear. It wasn't 100 percent effective, but after that, I only choked about once a month."

In my years of researching why golfers and other athletes choke under pressure, after interviewing hundreds of professional and amateur golfers, I believe that Dr. Cookson's plight is not uncommon — dramatic, perhaps, but common enough.

Golfers choke for a variety of reasons, but the number one cause is worrying too much about what other people will think if they fail, making them self-conscious and setting off their nervous systems. There is even a word for the fear of others' opinions: allodoxaphobia.

Most golfers probably do not need an appointment with a hypnotist or a psychologist, but they do need to get their peers out of their heads, whether it is their playing partners, their buddies back in the clubhouse who will eventually find out their score or the absent parent they are still trying to please. Many golfers tell me they get most nervous in crowded situations: on the first tee, on other holes where groups get backed up on the course, or on the ninth and 18th greens. In all those instances, groups of people are usually watching them. Little wonder that during such occasions, balls dribble off the tee and putts come up short.

"I guess these things have a lot to do with what other people think, of fear of failing in front of them," says Mary Ann Lapointe of Georgetown, Ontario, a five-time winner of the Ontario Amateur Ladies Championship. "It makes your body tight, and results in self-doubt and indecision."

Several times in his PGA Tour career, Peter Jacobsen's game suffered when he started worrying about what TV broadcasters thought of his swing. "I had to fix my swing so a broadcaster couldn't criticize it on national television," he said. "My rabbit ears affected my brain and as a result I didn't play well."

Golf teacher Fred Shoemaker of Carmel Valley, California, choked in a match against an amateur when he became afraid of what others would think if he lost. "What would people think of me?" he said. "What would my friends say? Think of the embarrassment! I abandoned my original goal of enjoying the experience. My goal became to beat this guy. I began to behave as most competitors: more distant, more separate from the situation. And I screwed up my own performance."

Amateurs get afraid, too. "People come to the golf course with the often unconscious fear that they will perform poorly, that they will disappoint, and even that they will be the subject of unspoken ridicule," says Phil Lee, a clinical instructor in psychiatry at Weill Medical College at Cornell University; Lee helps golfers with performance enhancement. But once golfers see others occasionally flub their shots, it takes some of the social pressure off, he adds. "It's almost a relief to realize that part of the pleasure we take in the poor shots of others has nothing to do with delighting in their misery and everything to do with removing them from the *higher than us* and *looking down on us* position that we have imagined them to occupy."

As we saw in the case of Dr. Cookson, this reaction can become rigidly set in a person's psyche, so that he or she repeatedly chokes in pressure situations, even though Mom is not in the foursome, and even when playing with complete strangers. When Greg Norman, the PGA Tour's career leading money-winner until 1999, began investigating why he was choking so often in major tournaments, some people told him he was trying too hard; perhaps he was set in a mode, from childhood, of trying to prove things to his stern father. "Even when I started climbing the ladder [in pro golf], he didn't think I'd be anything," Norman said. "I had a point to prove to him, to everybody."

Let's face it, we don't need other people to screw up our golf game; with the difficult technique of the swing and the amount of luck out there on the course, and with the self-doubts that seem to come with human nature, we can do that all by ourselves. As a human species, we have evolved into creatures of insecurity whose fears have changed drastically over the centuries from fear of dangerous animals to fear of what other people think. Partly this is nature's way of motivating us to survive, but it causes considerable self-destructive anxiety along the way.

It *is* possible to get frustrated while playing alone, of course, if you develop a glitch in your swing and keep repeating the problem. Frustration is a special kind of fear we will discuss in Chapter 5. Even then, it may still be about other people who will eventually find out about our score or our broken game. In general terms, however, most golfers report less tension in their swing when they are playing alone or on the practice range. That could be because they are not immediately distracted by other people or by their score. On the range, they are not nearly as self-conscious.

THE EXCUSES GAME

Yes, too many of us (count me in this group) worry about others in our foursome. That's probably one reason we offer excuses, before, during or after a round:

- "I've hardly played this year."
- "I really do need new shafts."
- "I haven't been getting enough sleep lately."
- "One of these days, I'm going to take lessons."

As we go deeper into this subject, let us not confuse choking with *bad golfing*. There is a difference between lousy technique and a swing affected by emotions and defensive psyche. Also, just because Greg Norman makes a poor shot once in a while doesn't mean he choked. But he may choke when he worries about the potential result of a shot and his muscles tense up.

In golf, letting other people *choke you* is a huge issue. If you could change one thing to improve your game, it should not be to correct your slice off the tee or to sharpen your chipping, but to *please* stop worrying about what other people think of your game, at least when you are at the golf course. If you can stop that, you'll not only get more enjoyment, but you'll be more mentally and physically relaxed, able to learn more quickly about techniques.

Jaime Diaz, a golf writer for *Sports Illustrated*, finds himself choking more often when he's in the company of golfers much better than he. "On those occasions when I would have to exhibit my game in front of the pros I wrote about, I turned into tapioca," he wrote. "In such a state I once nearly whiffed in view of Davis Love III, flailed helplessly before Lanny Wadkins and whizzed a shank under the nose of Corey Pavin, rendering each of them speechless."

Another time at a pro-am game, TV broadcaster Roger Maltbie told Diaz that a live camera was coming on just as he prepared to shoot. "My hands started sweating so badly that I didn't think I'd be able to hold on to the club," Diaz said. "My last thought before everything went blank was a pitiful prayer that somehow, some way, metal would make contact with a ball. When the earth began to rotate again, I saw my half-topped dribbler roll to a stop to my right … I'm a serial choker."

Another amateur golfer, Ron Gropp, says his fear of others has prevented him from entering tournaments. The 47-year-old Gropp, a seven-handicapper from Mississauga, Ontario, says he feels at home with a golf club in his hand, "but I have a fear. I am very shy and I try too hard in a tournament to impress people. To be honest, I have cried many times over this."

Hall of Fame Worriers

Don't fret, Ron, you've got some hall-of-fame company. Jack Nicklaus occasionally gets self-conscious, too, and embarrassed by bad shots or performances. Nicklaus says, "My urge for self-improvement has very little to do with winning, and nothing at all to do with making money or other materialistic factors. I've always believed that performances take care of those things. Any time that there's a cooling off in this impulse to improve, one emotion above all others will get a good blaze going again. It's embarrassment. I am very easily embarrassed by myself. No single emotion is more responsible for whatever I've achieved."

If it is any consolation to the rest of us, professional golf is riddled with stories of highly skilled players choking because they were worried about what others thought. In the 1955 U.S. amateur, the 15-year-old Nicklaus was rolling to victory when his golf idol Bobby Jones suddenly pulled up in a golf cart to watch. Jack bogeyed the next three holes, worried about what Jones would think if he made a bad shot — and the self-fulfilling prophecy came true. Greg Norman, worried partly about the media criticizing him for blowing yet another major tournament, let his emotions get the better of him and became too aggressive, frittering away a big lead in the final nine holes of the 1996 Masters. And who can forget Jean Van de Velde triple-bogeying the final hole of the 1999 British Open when he needed just a double-bogey to win? He refused to play safe and went for the flag, he later said, "because that's not the way Frenchmen play." Why would he worry about what people thought about a Frenchman's bravado? Next time, he may be advised to lay up with a wedge.

Of course, we can forgive pros for choking from time to time with the incredible pressures of their profession, with millions watching on TV, catching every angle, every facial expression, every misplay.

The big problem with worrying about what others think is that it makes us self-conscious. We become distracted by our worry of failure or even about the mechanics of our swing. And as soon as we start to worry or feel fear, it automatically sets off our mind-body's *emergency fear system* (one of two branches of our fear defence system, *see* Chapter 2), sending powerful hormones such as adrenaline, dopamine and endorphins throughout our brain and our muscles. We all know the emergency fear system well; it kicks in many times during a day in the form of stress at home or work. In the following two chapters, we will examine the emergency fear system and how we set it off while defending our ego and pride.

Yet the emergency fear system can sometimes help our golf game. Pros have shown they can sometimes perform better when they have something to prove to other people. With the outcome of the 1958 Masters in the balance, Arnold Palmer faced a tough shot on a par five hole when suddenly his old hero — none other than the beloved Bobby Jones once more — came up in his golf cart. "That made me nervous as hell, but I wanted to show him what I was made of," Palmer said years later. "So I took out a three-wood and smashed my second shot to the green. I made a 20-foot eagle putt and won." What was the difference in results between Nicklaus and Palmer while faced with Mr. Jones? It may have been that Palmer was just able to focus better that day, or it could have been that he was more experienced with such pressure than Nicklaus, who was younger at that point in his career.

Sometimes we choke (or rise to the occasion) because of our *own* expectations. "My nerves do not appear to be a result of concerns of what other people may think about my performance, but rather what I will think about my performance and my ego," says sports psychologist Gary Golbesky, who hopes one day to play on the Champions Tour, formerly the Senior PGA Tour. "I believe the higher the competitive level golfers reach, the more self-evaluation comes into play."

The best pros seem to form their own expectations, but only to a point. While Tiger Woods says he plays to meet his own criteria (and there is little evidence to doubt him), he also admits that in the big picture, he cares what other pros think about him. When he received an award as the best athlete of 1999, he said, "As an athlete, that's what you strive for — to have your peers respect your abilities in your sport."

And so, in review, we may be conscious of our need to impress others, or this issue may be semiconscious or subconscious. Remember that David Cookson, a doctor, needed professional therapy before he realized what was going on. Our own choking or yips may not be as deep, or as difficult to fix. We'll examine how to get at them in the final three sections of this book.

"Golf is a game of violence played from within."

—Dean Atkinson, director of golf,
Predator Ridge Golf Resort, Vernon, B.C.

CHAPTER 2

HEART BEATING FAST:
A Golfer's Primitive Defence System

Have your fingers ever trembled slightly when you put the ball on the tee for the first shot of the day? Have you found it difficult to focus or remain relaxed for a three-foot putt for par? Or just prior to a round against a worthy opponent, did your stomach flutter? If you have felt these things — and what golfer has not from time to time? — the cause for each of them is fear. Every time you feel nervous on the golf course, you are afraid. If you can accept this statement, if you can swallow this admission, you have accomplished much as a golfer. This awareness, this admission that you get afraid from time to time, is as important as learning to hit the ball straight up the middle. Even Tiger Woods admits to getting a little nervous; he knows that when our emergency hormones fill our body, we become in a way different people. This awareness, of course, makes him a better player.

Tension is a common indicator of fear. When a person feels tense, no matter what he or she is doing, it is almost always a result of the emergency fear system kicking in, according to Robert E. Thayer, professor of psychology at California State University, Long Beach, and a leading authority on emotions and moods. About the only other time this occurs in humans is when internally generated pain or allergic reactions produce a state of tension, he said.

These reactions to situations are hardwired into our nervous systems from millions of years ago, but the emergency fear system has taken some strange twists and turns as we have evolved from animals into more sophisticated beings. In the past 100 years, the challenge for humans who play golf has been to adapt this powerful, complex fear system into such a fragile game. It remains a work in progress.

In the big picture, nature has equipped us with many effective systems of defence against outside threats: everything from an immune system that protects us from disease to eyelids that close 20,000 times a day to repel dirt. Fear is one of our greatest defence systems. Its basic function is to help us overcome threatening situations, but if trained properly, fear can become an effective *offensive* weapon in competition. According to Boston psychiatrist Edward M. Hallowell, "Fear is at the core of our human experience — more than joy, anger, sadness and even love. Every cell in our body and each of our physiological systems can contribute in one way or another to our fear response."

The Emergency Fear System

Our fear defence system deals with two forms: long-term worry and short-term emergency fear. Emergency fear is our knee-jerk reaction to a sudden threat, be it an automobile accident, a public speaking engagement or a golfing opponent. To deal with such threats, we have the emergency fear system, which at its highest level of arousal produces a response known as fight or flight, providing maximum power, speed and concentration. The emergency fear system is capable of saving lives, but when it is activated for the wrong reasons each day, it can cause tension, poor performance and even illness. More often than not, it is the enemy of our golf game.

When we fear something on the golf course, whether it is fear of topping the ball or fear of what other people think, our emergency fear system kicks in, to allow more strength and sharpened concentration. But if this fear response is too great to control, our concentration and skills will suffer. We must learn how to tap these powers for positive use, and as you will see in Sections 2 through 4, we can.

Traditionally, fear is something we've been told we must avoid, especially on the golf course. We must not fall into this way of thinking. It is the way we cope with fear that needs improving. Says author Geoff Thompson, an expert on crisis situations, "What most people fail to realize is that whether you are facing a big business deal, a showdown with the boss or a couple of muggers, you will feel fear. We have to help people break down the prison walls by educating people in the histrionics of fear; how to recognize, understand and subsequently control and/or employ fear as an ally."

In golf, awareness of fear's mechanics is important, and admitting that you feel it is the first large step toward controlling it. Some of us might admit to feeling nervous or stressed, but, in order to come to grips with this problem, you need to admit to yourself that it is raw fear. And you need to address fear from the right angle.

The Amazing Hormones

Fear and other emotions stimulate the production of hormones, chemical substances that act as fuel and regulators in the mind and body. As well as their role in reacting to emergencies, hormones regulate a number of functions, including body growth, food use, sex and reproduction. They also provide the tension — as well as the excitement and happy feelings — in golfers. The brain contains some 10,000 hormones, and the duties of many of those remain unclear. Adrenaline is the most dramatic and widely known hormone activated during high arousal. It is generally a short-term chemical that causes energy peaks and valleys, and it can have negative effects. When golfers report the effects of adrenaline, they may actually be feeling the effects of dopamine and endorphin. Other hormones, such as cortisol, which have helped humans for

CHEMICAL	EFFECT
adrenaline	Increases heart and respiration rates, widens air passages, increases blood pressure and muscle tension. Overrated and often capable of more harm than good.
cortisol	A long-term hormone that prolongs adrenaline and noradrenaline. High levels can damage brain cells and accelerate aging.
DHEA	Promotes well-being and joy and reduces anxiety. Gives added energy.
dopamine	The body's rocket fuel, from which many other hormones follow. It stimulates aggression and awareness, co-ordinates muscle movement and speeds up thinking.
endorphin	A powerful painkiller, produced by the hypothalamus in the brain, it's the body's natural morphine. Suspected to produce "runner's high," although there is dispute about that.
noradrenaline	Similar to adrenaline in increasing heart rate and muscle activity. Improves alertness and reaction time. Strengthens willpower.
oxytocin	Promotes social bonding and teamwork.
serotonin	The neurotransmitter of inner peace. Linked with self-esteem, confidence and the ability to concentrate. Creates relaxation and happiness.
testosterone	A fight, but not a flight response, bringing strength, speed and power to maximum levels. Enhances the will to dominate an opponent.

thousands of years in their journey to find food, shelter and clothing, can stay in the system for weeks or months.

When golfers are faced with challenge, their emotional reactions send their minds and bodies through a series of chemical changes to help them deal with the situation. Among other things, it involves the central nervous system and adrenal glands as the heart rate, muscles, energy levels and concentration are (ideally) brought to their most effective levels (although over-arousal can impede performance). Indeed, when our emergency fear system kicks in, we become different people. The following table contains some of the hormones involved in this complicated process. Scientists are learning new things about them every day, and that some are pumped from the adrenal glands and others directly from neurotransmitters.

HOW IT'S TRIGGERED

Mostly through fear and sometimes anger. It's more of a defensive "flight" fuel.

When a golfer feels anxiety, anger, guilt, frustration.

Released in the endocrine system by positive, loving thoughts. Golfers sometimes raise it with thoughts of loved ones at times of crisis.

From challenge. It responds to positive thinking more than adrenaline does and speeds up momentum.

By pain and other fight-or-flight feelings.

When a golfer turns to aggression in a competitive situation. It's more of a "fight" fuel than adrenaline.

By thinking of achievements and goals as a team rather than in an individual sense.

Thorough appreciative feelings toward teammates. Stretching, walking, low-impact aerobics and meditative martial arts boost its levels.

Through a very competitive mind-set and strong desire to overcome an opponent.

Think and Grow Tense

Hormones are extremely sensitive to the brain's thought processes. One of the enormous issues we have not addressed properly in golf, let alone in society itself, is that we think too much. Through evolution, human beings have become thinking machines. Research shows that the average person has 66,000 thoughts per day. Hardly a waking moment goes by (never mind during sleep) when we are not thinking about something. In our evolution, anthropologists and other experts in human behaviour say, the human mind has become our strongest resource. It has become more powerful than our muscles, taking control over much of our daily lives. But our fear defence system is far behind our sophisticated brains and if we are not careful, it can be triggered by thoughts alone. That is why we must lessen our thoughts on the golf course, to stop these physical caveman responses from interfering with our swing and our decision-making. Even simple distractions through thinking can be fatal on a nine-iron approach to the green.

It has been well-documented that thinking can lead to stress and distraction with the delicate golf swing. "When your mind is cluttered, your body usually reacts by tensing up," says golf teacher David Leadbetter.

Golf psychologist Mark Shatz calls this "monkey mind" and says it is more prevalent with beginners. "The mind's wandering tendencies, combined with ugly golfing skills, causes the bad golfer's mind to leap from mechanical concerns to thoughts of gloom and doom to insignificant worries," he said.

Jessica Maxwell, a golfing beginner and author of *Driving Myself Crazy*, agrees that too many *"swing thoughts"* ruin her game: "A dark funnel of advice begins twisting in my head. Read the ball. Keep your eye on the back of the ball. Keep your head still. Keep your head in the club head. Let the club do the work. Let your hands work together. Use your big muscles. Visualize your shot ... but don't force it. Holy moley."

Over-thinking can even cause headaches. "I'm tired in my head because I've been thinking a lot," said Swedish LPGA star Annika Sorenstam. "Having to make all those decisions on the course can tire you out mentally."

Believe it or not, even too many *good* thoughts before a swing can be harmful if they get you so elated that the emotions affect your muscles and coordination. But by far the most harmful thoughts of all are worries and self-doubt. *Fear* thoughts. It's estimated that two-thirds of the 66,000 thoughts per day are negative. What else have you done in your life 44,000 times, never mind in one day? Thinking about what could go wrong — a bad shot or the consequences of a bad shot on your scorecard — often acts as a self-fulfilling prophecy, as your fear defence system kicks in with its rushing hormones and your wayward shot ends up in the rough.

Worry: Your Other Fear System

Worry is separate from emergency fear, yet it often interacts with emergency fear and influences the way we react to pressure. When a sudden threat arises, the size of our response may be influenced by how much we have already been worrying about the potential threat. For instance, if I am playing poorly with a three-wood off the fairway, I tend to worry about it ahead of time. And so, even before I stand over the ball, my emergency fear system starts to act up.

Just as emergency fear employs the emergency fear system as its major resource, worry has the *worry system*. The worry system has a broad range of resources, more elaborate than those of the emergency fear system, which primarily uses fear and anger. Fear is at the base of the worry system, but other emotions have time to come into the powerful mix, including love, sadness, jealousy and hope. Worry uses the hormone cortisol, which has a number of benefits and can stay in your body for weeks, but it can make you sick if you fret too much. However, when we worry constructively about an upcoming game, we can summon our energy, willpower, talent and strategy. But most of the time, we worry when there is no danger. Let me put it another way: most of the time we fear when there is no danger.

After the third round of the 2002 Rochester International, Mi Hyun Kim held a comfortable five-stroke lead until she started to fret that the weather might turn bad and ruin her chances of victory. "I couldn't sleep [the night before the final round]. I was just thinking too much and watching the Weather Channel." The weather did get a little windy the next day, but it was Kim's fatigue that did her in, and she opened the final round with a three-putt bogey and finished the day with a 74 to squander the lead.

"Worry was intended to be a useful, built-in alarm system," says Boston psychiatrist Edward M. Hallowell, an occasional golfer and author of several self-help books. "Not all worry is bad. Effective planning depends on anticipating danger. This is worry at its best. The trick is to learn to worry well, at the right time, to the right degree."

Emotional Drive: Within the worry system is an important resource that I call *emotional drive.* Simply put, it is our will to survive. In the broadest sense, it is life itself. Without that will there is not much point having muscles and other physical defences. Some people may call this determination. We are determined to survive, so we do whatever it takes, and the human species has certainly proven formidable in the face of many serious threats over the centuries. I believe emotional drive is often activated through healthy worry. Sometimes you can feel your emotional drive in the energy you have, perhaps a restlessness, particularly when you are provoked or challenged. It seems to be saying, "Let's go, let's go!" Some people call this nervous energy, and I believe worry and insecurity often set it off.

More about healthy worry and emotional drive in Chapter 11.

Pressure and Stress

Pressure is a term used often in golf. We say we're feeling pressure in a competition, or while attempting an important shot. When we feel tensed-out, we call it stress. But what do these terms mean to our golf game? Pressure and stress have become clichéd and oversimplified to the point that we find it hard to identify the problems they present, or how to work through them. It will help if we identify them as both being based from fear.

Let's separate them:

Pressure: It is the demand we feel to produce. This pressure comes from one of three sources: it may be *external* (when we face a tough match or tournament), *psychological* (from worry or from expectations from others or ourselves) or *emotional* (when we get frustrated, we feel more pressure and more frustration).

Fear reaction: Our fear defence system kicks in whenever we feel pressure, either the emergency fear system or the worry system. The greater we perceive the threat to be, the more our mind-body will change with its rush of energy and potent hormones.

Stress: It is the mental and/or physical reaction we feel when the fear defence system is triggered, such as tension or butterflies. If the stress becomes unmanageable and counterproductive, we call it *distress*. (Continually feeling distressed can make us ill.) If we are able to channel the nervous energy into productive use in our game, we call it *eustress*.

Put in another way, both pressure and stress are connected to the thoughts and sensations we feel when we react with fear to a threat.

The threats may be fear of missing a shot or deeper issues regarding fear of failure or fear of what other people think about us, or at least about our golf game. In 2002, I came across a man from Alberta who actually had a fear of hitting houses along the golf course with his ball, because he had done it so many times. PGA player Ian Leggatt says that at one time he had to overcome the *fear of winning* and all of the responsibilities and pressures that can bring. That can also happen to amateurs, such as Theresa Coleman, a member at Lambton Golf and Country Club in Toronto. "People tell me I have a good swing and I'm a very good putter," she says. "But I play differently on the course than I do on the range; I don't trust my swing. I've thought a lot about it. Maybe I'm afraid to get good. Maybe I'm afraid to succeed."

Leggatt, who went on to win the 2002 Touchstone Tucson Open, and Coleman are ahead of the psychology game because many of us do not want to hear that we may be afraid of something. We'll admit to being pressured or stressed, all right. But afraid? Of what? Our competition? Our neighbour down the street? Naw, how can we be afraid of those guys, or what they think? Isn't fear a sign of weakness? But maybe sometimes we are afraid. It can be a very natural reaction. Even the towering figures of the world of sport — Tiger Woods, Michael Jordan, Martina Hingas and Ted Turner — all admit to being afraid from time to time. Aren't these the most confident people in their fields? Yes, but they have learned that fear is a way of life in competitive or social situations and that it can actually help them perform better.

It's the same thing with pressure. How many of us equate pressure with fear? We're not afraid, we say, we're just feeling a little bit of pressure.

If you *think* something is important — like a shot out of a sand trap on No. 18 — you will likely set off your emergency fear system with its hormonal chemicals triggering increased muscle activity and tension. Some people call this *fear energy,* the fuel of the emergency fear system. "Your emotions affect every cell in your body," says Thomas Tutko, a pioneer sports psychologist at San Jose State University, who has consulted for many professional athletes.

Fear reaction often turns to distress if the demands placed upon us are too great for us to handle, or too great for our resources. In other words, if you are a high handicapper always expecting to improve your score, a tough golf course may produce unreasonable demands. If you usually expect to reach a green in two shots, long holes may produce too much pressure onto your game and you may get distressed. That's when your game tends to break down.

We may be more susceptible to pressure, fear reaction and stress at some times than others, depending on our mood and our energy level. (In Section II, we will discuss ways to keep pressure

FIGHT, FLIGHT, FAKE OR FREEZE

When the emergency fear system activates to its maximum, it is called the fight-or-flight response. The cliché definition for fight or flight is that you either fight the threat or run away from it. But I believe there are at least two other reactions between those opposite responses: freezing up or pretending to get ready to fight.

When somebody freezes during a pressure situation, it is often described as panic, but that may be misleading in some cases. The freeze in our animal response is geared to make us less conspicuous to predators or threats we believe we cannot meet head-on or outrun. In some cases, we stop breathing so predators cannot hear us. This freeze period also gives us a chance to use strategy: should we try to fight or run?

The pretending-to-fight scenario is also common when we feel fear. Let's refer to it as fake. Fight, flight, freeze or fake. The fake in the natural response makes our hairs stand on end, so we look bigger before a potential fight with a foe or predator. That was useful in primitive times when we were covered with hair. We still feel it today when our hair tingles. LPGA legend Nancy Lopez has reported feeling her hair stand on end when she is in contention.

In golf, the freeze and fake scenarios are seen much more often than fight or flight, because punch-ups and running don't occur on the golf course, unless you get involved in links rage (see Chapter 5).

at manageable levels and keep golf an enjoyable activity.)

One reason we rarely use fear as an ally is that we avoid it; as soon as we feel fear's often uncomfortable feelings, we avoid it and try to get out of the pressure situation as quickly as possible.

Types of Alarms

We can break the mind-body's arousal response into "fire hall" terms, depending on the expected degree of challenge or threat that we feel in a situation. Here is an approximate comparison of the kind of situations we face, in life and on the links.

	IN LIFE:	IN GOLF:
One-Alarm	A phone call. Is it important?	Playing with friends in a non-competitive round.
Two-Alarm	A phone call in the middle of the night. You prepare for the unexpected.	Playing in a league match, but with the score in perspective.
Three-Alarm	A blow up at work; a domestic quarrel.	First tee jitters.
Four-Alarm	You are suddenly faced with losing your job.	Your self-esteem is wrapped up in your game while facing a match shot.
Five-Alarm	A mugger has you cornered.	An angry foe comes at you with a club or cart (it has happened).

"Our greatest need is to satisfy our egos.

It's the need we all have to feel important."

— William J. Beausay, *retired president of*
the Academy of Sports Psychology

CHAPTER 3

THE SOPHISTICATED EGO DEFENCE

If we are becoming more aware of what causes choking in golf, if we can start to admit some of our vulnerabilities, imagine this scenario:

As you walk a golf course, you are a lot like your cave ancestor of a million years ago. Like him, you are walking around beautiful nature with a club in your hand, looking for challenges. When a threat appears, you react the same way he did long ago: your emergency fear system gears up with its rushing hormones and pumped-up muscles. Suddenly, that club in your hand is a powerful weapon.

But the reason your body reacts in such a way has certainly changed over the distant ages. In his time, the caveman was staving off hunger by stalking a primitive pheasant, but now you are hunting a birdie of a different kind. You are defending your pride and reputation by keeping your score down; he was just protecting his physical existence on a harsh planet.

Yes, the threats to us have changed over the millennia, but our emergency fear system has not, which is one of the big issues in our golf game. At one time, our survival needs and our *primitive* fears were simpler than they are today. Long before golf and organized sports were invented, nature was worried about other types of competition — the competition to survive physically against predators, the weather, neighbouring tribes and famine. It was a full-time job to find food and shelter and to procreate. Nature introduced fear to inspire us in these areas, particularly when our needs were not being met. And to defend against these fears, nature equipped us with survival mechanisms, sometimes known as defence mechanisms. A prime example is the emergency fear system, and another is our physical attraction to one another, nature's survival mechanism for procreation.

As the human brain evolved, its worry system developed, helping us anticipate potential problems, such as a dogleg right.

The primitive needs, fears and survival/defence mechanisms are still with us today, but they are harder to detect. In primitive times, fears seemed bigger because in most cases we could actually see the source of the fear: saber-toothed tigers, mastodons and enemy tribes. In today's world, we rarely see our fears in 3-D, but we've developed more fears than we ever had, such as the fear of topping a little white ball. We are sophisticated animals, albeit a little confused in the way we allow ourselves to get nervous. Yes, our civilization and technology, our governments and safety nets, have removed much of the work for our physical needs. Yet fear and *healthy* worry remain our most potent weapons.

As our brains, egos and social structures have become more sophisticated, so have our priorities, fears and survival mechanisms. The threats to humans in our competition-based society have changed; the survival game has become more psychological and emotional, riddled with issues of status and society. One of the important things today is to *be somebody*. Those with standing are awarded the trophies and the attention. In a way, the game remains the survival of the fittest. Our strong needs are centred around self-esteem and ego, and out of those needs are born fears: fear of failure, fear of what others think about us and fear of loss of status, not to mention the fear of our scorecard being posted in the locker room. These fears increasingly take on greater importance because we have more time to think (and worry) than ever before. Our mind-bodies were made for *doing* more than thinking, but now we create mini-worlds in our heads, complete with characters and problems parallel to those in real life. Both doing and thinking are real to our nervous system and its 9-1-1 reactions, but our fear response will probably remain the same for another 100,000 years. When we fear a threat, even if it's just a family problem or a business affair, adrenaline and cortisol are pumped into our system to prepare for a fight or at least a physical response.

"We are still living in the bodies of our caveman ancestors in a world they never dreamed existed, and we will be for thousands of years to come," said the late Robert Eliot, former director of the Institute of Stress Medicine in Denver. "If they knew how we were using their adrenaline and endorphins, they'd be surprised. We have an arousal system designed to put us into physical activity under stress, but in our age we're invisibly trapped; all this energy gets turned inward and the 30 to 40 little challenges we face every day are turned into physiological stress. We don't need to respond to physical threats as much, but we get psyched up in response to someone's criticism or a driver who cuts us off on the way home from work or the report card that our son brings home from school."

Ego on the Links

In an individual sport like golf, pride sticks out like a flag on a green. Hence it is a fertile laboratory for studying the ego defence, which can be a potent yet unwieldy force in competitive golf — even in casual golf, if production means something to us.

In competitive sports in general, the ego defence dominates, for better or for worse. Carole Seheult, a British sports psychologist, has studied this subject — how athletes respond to situations with psychological and emotional reactions deeply set in their psyche. She refers to these reactions as defence mechanisms, and they can provide extra energy, intensity and determination at crucial times in a match. According to Seheult, "The area of competitive sport, particularly at the elite level, is likely to provide ample opportunity for the exercise of an individual's defence mechanisms. Head-to-head competition or involvement in major championships, where an athlete or player has to be prepared to put himself or herself on the line, to ask of themselves testing questions regarding levels of skill and commitment, and to extend limits of performance, will undoubtedly trigger instinctual feelings of anxiety against which the ego will need to protect itself. Further pressures may also come from external sources such as relationships with coaches, sponsors, officials and family, as well as internal feelings regarding rivals and opponents."

Such defence mechanisms include denial, repression and isolation. They can be proactive or negative, *adaptive* or *maladaptive*, resulting either in a successful performance or a self-destructive one. For example, when facing a tough match against a seemingly unbeatable foe, a golfer may react with denial. This denial may help the golfer maintain a high performance level because he or she is unafraid of the favoured opponent and does not accept the danger of losing, even when behind on the back nine of a tournament. That is the *adaptive* reaction. The *maladaptive* reaction would be for the golfer not to understand the challenge in the skilled opponent and fail to make the required effort to win.

According to Seheult, these defence mechanisms are often subconscious, automatic reactions of the mind-body system, but becoming aware of them can enhance an athlete's performance. "A better understanding of the way an individual athlete is likely to respond in situations such as trials, qualifying competitions for major championships, or even Olympic finals can only be regarded as useful," she said.

Psychologists say these defence mechanisms — the way a golfer learns to react to stressful situations — can be shaped in childhood, adolescence or in the highly competitive world of sports. When a golfer or any competitive athlete defends pride or ego, it often unleashes anger and fear, and those are the greatest boosters of powerful hormones, says Yuri Hanin, a pioneer Russian sports researcher, now professor and senior researcher at the Research Institute for Olympic Sports in Finland. In fact, many professional and international athletes are not as successful as their opponents because they don't tap into the so-called "negative" emotions, such as aggression, fear and anxiety. Hanin says, "High-level mobilizing energy comes from negative emotions; they are often untouched reserves. Positive emotions (joy and contentment) are not as quick to act or as intensive as negative emotions. Not all athletes are ready for competitions because they don't have enough negatives, or they don't channel or allocate them in the right way." In his research, Hanin has found that about 40 percent of elite athletes need a high level of pre-competition anxiety to perform well. "They are more efficient when they're tense or nervous. That's helpful to them."

These nervous feelings are often the product of the mind-body's fear defence system, Hanin said. "It's a type of defence, a response to a threat. The whole person reacts, not just the mind or body. It's a holistic response. The successful [athletes] are those able to establish a clear link between the uncomfortable feelings and what has triggered them, and then act on it." Hanin added that the fear defence system can be genetic, originating from a human's primal programming, but it can also be learned from childhood or through the world of competitive sports.

In golf, the ego defence often kicks in when players defend their ego or pride, according to Patrick J. Cohn, a sports psychologist who works with golfers on the PGA, LPGA, Nationwide and Asian tours. "When you feel fear about missing a short putt to win a match, the increase in adrenaline, heart rate, blood pressure and respiration function to prepare your body and mind for action," he says in his book, *The Mental Game of Golf*. "Since you're never in physical danger when you play golf, the anxiety you experience is triggered by a perception of threat to your self-esteem or ego. The increased adrenaline you experience when trying to avoid a car accident is very helpful to your safety. When you get scared over making a five-foot putt for par, excess tension only ruins a fluid stroke. The worry, fear and tentativeness you feel about missing a putt is not an abnormal reaction in that situation, but if you don't learn to control your emotions in that situation, anxiety gets the best of you. Everyone has similar feelings under stress, but what separates a person who chokes from the person who copes is how he deals with those feelings."

Golf is an excellent sport to study the effects of pride and ego. Without self-consciousness, without ego, there is no competitive golf, perhaps no golf at all. As long as score is kept, golfers will have expectations and, when cards are compared, ego comes into play. Without this, there can be little bravado during battle in a sport with no teammates to rely on.

This brings us back to the fear defence system, which can kick in if we believe our ego is threatened by a bad shot or by our opponents. What will others think about us if our game sucks? It is human nature to ask this question, if only subconsciously, and then it is automatic nature for our emergency fear system to activate with its rushing hormones, increased blood pressure and heart rate. Our nervous system has problems determining what is a real or perceived threat, what is a threat to our safety or just one to our ego. When our ego defence surfaces, the emergency fear system kicks in and we become aroused, to either feel more powerful, or weaker and more vulnerable. Most often it is the latter. Think of how you feel on the first tee. You haven't played a hole yet, so you may not trust your swing, especially with other duffers lined up behind you. Your worry can cause tension and a halted swing, and suddenly Mr. Titleist disappears into the tall grass.

THE THREAT OF A TIGER

The threat of Tiger Woods has wounded some egos on the PGA Tour in recent years. Like many other talented pros, whenever Davis Love III or Phil Mickelson see Woods challenging for the lead, they seem to freeze (that's the primitive human response to a predator: to stop dead so he will not be noticed). Although some golfers self-destruct in public, many keep their self-esteem issues well-hidden or they use the experience to show their character or calmness in the eye of a storm. Due to the fair-play nature of the game, you must respect and honour your opponent as much as yourself. Exceptions are such competitions as the Ryder Cup and the Solheim Cup, when elite golfers often come out of their individual shells to let the testosterone flow for their teammates.

Some of the world's best can thrive — or crash — when their pride is threatened. Remember from Chapter 1 the different reactions of Jack Nicklaus and Arnold Palmer when Bobby Jones rode up in a cart to watch them? Often great athletes like Palmer and Nicklaus thrive in pressure situations when they are defending their egos, says clinical psychologist Robert W. Grant, who wrote a book on the subject, *The Psychology of Sport: Facing One's True Opponent*. They have been defending themselves so often from a young age, they achieve by overcompensating for psychological issues, he said. "Motivators such as fun are not enough to push and sustain elite athletes through the painful gauntlet that must be run to reach the top," Grant said. "Success usually brings a great deal of material from which one can create or repair a damaged ego or enhance an already stable and strong identity." In serious competitions, it usually boils down to self-preservation of the ego, Grant said. And Tiger Woods agrees: "I love feeling the pressure; I love it. I was telling my dad, 'There's no better position than being up front.' Everyone is looking at you and you get all the pressure in the world. You can go nowhere but down."

And so, used constructively, a little ego in the bag can lower your score, unless you let it get in the way of self-honesty, camaraderie and your development as a golfer.

OTHER DEFENCES AND MOTIVATORS

Although the ego defence can dominate golf competition, there are other things we defend as golf animals.

Golfers and other athletes sometimes defend a group. The histories of the Solheim, Ryder and President's cups are filled with tales of golfers producing remarkable performances in the name of their nation. In amateur play, the same thing can happen when a champion is representing a club at a tournament. Such defences also seem related to our strong desire to protect our territory. That has also come into play somewhat with golfers Lee Elder and Notah Begay III feeling they are playing partly to represent their race. Then there was Jack Nicklaus, playing partly for the senior set in winning the 1986 Masters, when he got angry because some members of the media said he was too old to win another major.

Some pro golfers play better when they feel they are protecting their loved ones by earning a good living, and others simply admit they are materialistic in their motives, like Byron Nelson, who won 11 consecutive PGA tournaments in 1945. He recalled of his early years: "My dream was to own a ranch. Golf was the only way I was going to get that ranch. And every tournament I played in, I was going after a piece of it. First I had to buy some property. Then I had to fence it. Then I had to build a house for it ... then I had to put enough money aside to take care of it forever. That was what I won tournaments for. It's amazing, but once I got that ranch all paid for, I pretty much stopped playing. I was all but done as a competitive player."

In this complicated issue of human achievement and failure, we may want to describe our drive to succeed as a motivation rather than a defence mechanism. The two may be interrelated, psychologists say. They generally break motivation down into two areas: intrinsic (internal) and extrinsic (external). Examples of intrinsic motivators are challenge or excitement of the game or the achievement of goals, while extrinsic motivators are things like social approval from peers or playing for big contracts and trophies. According to William J. Beausay, athletes are influenced by seven motivations, often in combination of several at one time:

- **Money**. "It's a heck of a motivator early in a career (especially to provide for family), but becomes less so as an athlete makes more and more."
- **Ego**. "It's the need we all have to feel important. In psychology, we say 'You never get enough of that wonderful stuff.' That usually means sex, but that's actually No. 2. Our greatest need is to satisfy our egos."
- **Camaraderie**. "It feels good to be one of the guys."
- **Expectations**. "They feel like they must live up to the expectations of others."
- **Achievement**. "Some athletes simply have an innate need to get things done."
- **Excellence**. "It's a need to be the best at what you do."
- **Love of the game**. "Some athletes just love what they do so much, they can't give it up."

"I don't know what happened on that three-

footer. I think my hands shaking may have

had something to do with it."

— Angela Buzminski after missing an easy putt to send the
American General Futures Classic of 2000 (on the SBC Futures Tour)
to a playoff. She regained her composure to win the tournament.

CHAPTER 4

THE IMPACT OF PRESSURE:
Sundays in the Garden of Evil

O kay, we've established that everybody has an emergency fear system that kicks in many times a day, to varying degrees, when we feel threatened or frustrated. Let's search for a sporting event to plug our emergency fear system into. We must keep in mind that, when aroused, the increase in heart rate caused by the emergency fear system tends to hinder complex tasks and those involving small muscles and fine motor skills. But it can improve tasks involving bigger muscles and power skills.

Rigorous physical sports such as boxing, hockey and football seem to be the activities affected by our primitive impulses towards self-defence and the accompanying release of energy. Our emergency fear system was made for action, which translates well in these high-octane, sometimes violent games. We can even fight or flee from time to time. Basketball isn't such a bad working environment, either. But there is little chance for physical release in golf, unless you are letting fly a powerful shot with a wood.

Besides golf, baseball is another dangerous turf for high arousal.

A study revealed that home teams lose more often than not in a seventh World Series game because of fielding errors, perhaps caused by nerves under high expectations. The nature of golf, with its intricate mechanics, distractions and vulnerability to overthinking, is about as compatible to our central nervous system as booze.

THE NEUROTIC GAME

For such an aesthetically beautiful sport, golf contains a minefield. Look at all the worrisome distractions and pitfalls it offers (you may come up with a few of your own):

- The small room for error in the swing.
- The difficulty of golf courses, especially ones you are not familiar with.
- The difficulty of becoming proficient without constant play or practice.
- The lack of physical action and thus little release for the buildup of tension.
- Weather conditions.
- The distraction of playing partners who are too good, too bad or simply rude.
- The amount of time between shots in which to think and worry.
- The solitary nature of the game, with ego coming to the fore, with all its trappings, including the worry of others watching you.
- The emphasis on score.
- The time and expense it takes to play the game.
- The mental and physical drain of a four- to five-hour game.

Architects such as Robert Trent Jones may have constructed golf courses, but sometimes it seems as if Lucifer himself designed the game. And when you combine two of the most sensitive things on earth, the human mind and golf, you have the potential for minor miracles, but more often for mayhem (don't despair, the miracles part is detailed in the following chapter).

To find examples of choking, we don't have to look far. One day over a drink in your clubhouse, start up a conversation about the subject and, if your colleagues are truthful, stories will abound. Everyone may have a different definition of choking and, in fact, there seem to be many different ways to choke on the golf course: seizing up, trying too hard, getting too elated, overcompensating for an earlier shank or being under-aroused.

"Everybody chokes," says PGA legend Tom Watson. "You just try to choke the least." Anecdotes of choking on the pro golf tours are more common than stories of great rounds and finishes. You hear more about how players lose tournaments than win.

"The guy who wins a golf tournament isn't the guy who hits the greatest amount of good shots, but the guy who hits the least amount of bad shots," says Gary Cowan, Canada's amateur male golfer of the last century. (Some bad shots, of course, have nothing to do with choking, but under pressure they often do.)

Even superstars like Tiger Woods and Annika Sorenstam choke from time to time. Not much is written about Sunday scoring averages, how professional players score on the final day of a tournament. There have been few, if any, inventories on how competitors score in the clutch. Little wonder. Golfers generally don't like to talk much about such painful issues as the way pressure affects their game. Perhaps that is one reason golfers do not improve as much as they would like to.

But here is the painful truth: my research shows that on the final day of a tournament, most players choke, or at least play worse as the pressure is pumped up a notch. In other words, they let their doubts and emotions interfere with their skills. Even the best among us are sufferers. During his 1999 PGA Tour season, Woods probably succumbed to pressure more than he conquered it. His Sunday scoring average was 70.85, nearly two full strokes worse than his Thursday-through-Saturday score, 68.86. Of course, his rivals had more meltdowns than he did and he won eight tournaments. But Woods got better on Sundays in the next two years and, over the first six years of his career (1996–2001), his final-day average was 69.57 strokes, just slightly higher than his average for the other rounds.

In any career lasting five years or more, few PGA or LPGA players have Sunday scoring averages better than their averages Thursday through Saturday. Of course, this is a complex topic, but experts and many players say pressure is the number one reason for the Sunday blues. So don't go picking on Greg Norman, because nobody else has been able to conquer nerves over the long haul, either — not Phil Mickelson, David Duval, Nancy Lopez or Juli Inkster.

Although pressure is usually tougher in the late going of a tournament, some golfers choke early on or when trying to make a cut. "The first round of the Masters has killed me for 15 straight years," former PGA star Johnny Miller once said.

Pressure to perform in front of home fans is another issue; a study of the British Open revealed that the scores of contending British players deteriorated more than those of contending foreign players from the first to the final rounds.

Some golfers, such as Frank Nobilo of the European and PGA Tours, don't want to talk about choking, while others are open about it. "I bled all over the place," said Blaine McCallister, explaining how he blew the 2000 Compaq Classic to Carlos Franco. In the 1999 B.C. Open, the PGA's most accurate driver, Fred Funk, tensed up on the first playoff hole, put his tee shot into the rough and lost to Brad Faxon. And sure, Nicklaus won 18 major championships, but he also finished second 19 times in the majors. Sweet-swinging Fred Couples seems to be one of golf's most relaxed competitors, but he admits, "On Sundays, extra nerves are involved."

In amateur golf, the feelings of fear and anger can embrace your game like two drunk uncles crashing your foursome. Such emotions can have as much effect on your game as the weather or your opponents at times, even more than your talent.

Putting and the short game seem most vulnerable to nerves because of the pressure to score and because the emergency fear system affects small muscles (hands and wrists) and complex shots. Even the brilliant Annika Sorenstam sometimes gets shaky, especially in major tournaments. From 1994 through 2001, the Swedish star had a lofty winning percentage of 19.8 percent — 28 wins in 141 non-major tournaments. But in the four majors over that time span, her percentage was just 10.3 percent (three of 29). She said of her troubles of 1998, "Once I got to the green, I couldn't see the hole. It felt like it was getting smaller and smaller. When you can't really make the putt, you start thinking, 'Do I need to do something else? Do I need to try another weapon?'"

In general terms, many skills involved in your golf game can benefit from low to medium levels of arousal. For example, when you are putting, you can generally stand your heart rate going up to 115 beats per minute, but after that the dexterity of your fingers is lessened. For an iron approach shot to the green, a complex motor skill involving a series of muscle groups and movements that require hand-eye coordination, precision, tracking and timing, you may be able to stand a heart rate of 145. Higher arousal (beyond 145) can actually help gross motor skills, such as a tee shot or a long blast with a fairway wood.

HITTING THE SOUR SPOT: DOCUMENTING THE CHOKES

No one can say for sure whether the following examples from pro golf were actually the result of choking, or just bad playing. But even seasoned professionals are affected by pressure:

- **1925 U.S. Open** — Bobby Jones blows a three-shot lead over the final six playoff holes to lose to unknown Willie Macfarlane.
- **1938 U.S. Open** — Ray Ainsley takes 19 strokes on one hole.
- **1939 U.S. Open** — Worried about being humiliated, Sam Snead's teeth chatter as he shoots eight on the final hole to lose. He never wins the Open.
- **1946 U.S. Open** — Ben Hogan misses a putt of less than three feet on the 72nd hole to miss a playoff by one stroke.
- **1956 Masters** — As an amateur, Ken Venturi shoots 80 in the final round to lose by one to Jackie Burke.
- **1966 Masters** — Arnold Palmer blows a seven-shot lead with nine holes remaining and loses to Billy Casper.
- **1967 Masters** — Peter Allis four-putts from five feet on the 11th green.
- **1970 British Open** — Doug Sanders gets angry at a fan, then freezes before missing a 30-inch putt on the 72nd hole, then loses a playoff to Jack Nicklaus.
- **1976 Bing Crosby National Pro-Am** — Flubbing his way around Pebble Beach, Jack Nicklaus shoots 82.
- **1979 Masters** — Ed Sneed bogeys the final three holes, then loses a playoff to Fuzzy Zoeller.
- **1980 Masters** — Tom Weiskopf puts five straight balls into the water on No. 12.
- **1986 Masters** — Corey Pavin lets the pond at No. 16 distract him and spoils his chances of winning.
- **1989 Masters** — Scott Hoch misses a two-foot putt in a playoff loss to Nick Faldo.
- **1989 U.S. Open** — Tom Kite blows the third-round lead with a triple-bogey and two double-bogeys.
- **1990 U.S. Women's Open** — Patty Sheehan blows a nine-shot lead over the final 27 holes to lose to Betsy King.
- **1991 Ryder Cup** — Mark Calcavecchia is four up over Colin Montgomerie,

then gets rattled and loses the final four holes. Bernhard Langer's four-foot miss loses for Europe.

- **1996 U.S. Open** — Davis Love III misses a three-footer on the 72nd hole to lose by one.
- **1996 Masters** — Greg Norman blows a six-shot lead in the final round to lose to Nick Faldo.
- **1997 British Open** — Partly distracted by a train, Tiger Woods takes a triple-bogey on No. 11.
- **1999 British Open** — Jean Van de Velde blows a three-shot lead on the final hole, then loses a playoff.
- **2000 Australian Ladies Masters** — Lorie Kane finishes second for the ninth time without a win, before finally breaking through with three victories.
- **2000 Firstar Classic** — Karrie Webb, angry about hitting into the bunker, takes a practice swing into the sand, incurring a two-shot penalty, and blows the tournament.
- **2001 Office Depot** — Pat Hurst bogeys six of the last 10 holes, allowing Annika Sorenstam to come from 10 strokes behind to overtake her for the victory.
- **2000 PGA Tour qualifying school** — After playing the first 16 holes of the final round in eight under, Tim O'Neal is four over for the last two holes, and fails to get his tour card.
- **2001 McDonald's LPGA Championship** — Laura Diaz is nervous only on the 72nd hole, missing a four-foot putt to lose to Karrie Webb.
- **2001 Buick Invitational** — Phil Mickelson double-bogeys the third playoff hole, but wins after Frank Lickliter three putts from 12 feet for a triple.
- **2001 International** — Chris DiMarco blows a six-point lead in the final round by going seven over in an eight-hole stretch.
- **2001 Toshiba Senior Classic** — Bob Gilder blows the lead by playing the last four holes of the front nine in seven over.
- **2001 Asahi Ryokuken International** — Kris Tschetter four putts a hole while tied for the lead in the final round, losing to Tina Fischer.
- **2001 U.S. Open** — Retief Goosen and Stewart Cink both miss two-foot putts while contending on the 72nd hole.

- **2002 AT&T Pebble Beach National Pro-Am** — Pat Perez, Andrew Magee and Lee Janzen all bogey the 72nd hole with a chance to win.
- **2002 British Open** — Thomas Levet unbelievably uses a wayward driver on two tight fairways coming in and loses a playoff to Ernie Els.
- **2002 PGA Championship** — Tiger Woods, obviously buckled by an eagle by eventual winner Rich Beem, bogeys two straight crucial holes on the back nine.
- **2002 Ryder Cup** — Phil Mickelson of the U.S., the world's second-ranked player and a 2–5 favourite, looks shaky in losing three and two to Phillip Price of Wales, ranked 119th in the world.

  NOTE: There are fewer documented chokes on the LPGA, which until recent years has not been as closely scrutinized as the PGA.

Arousal's Effect on Your Swing and Your Game

"I got my legs going too quick on the tee shot."

—Fred Funk, the PGA Tour's most accurate driver, describing how he "choked" on his drive on his way to losing a playoff.

Few people are born with a natural swing; they have to work at it. In fact, throwing the ball around a course, which some people do to get into the *Guinness Book of World Records*, is more natural to the human physique than hitting it with a club.

"Everyone knows that golf is a very unnatural game," said golf psychiatrist Phil Lee. "And anyone who forgets that has only to watch a good athlete play golf for the first time to be reminded of just how unnatural and difficult a game it is. The more natural the sport, the less the psychological interference." Michael Jordan, probably basketball's best ever and one of the game's most gifted athletes, is also a dedicated golfer. But he continues to struggle with golf. Says Jordan of his swing, "I've had a problem for some time with a closed club on top, and that causes me to hook. I'm a good enough athlete to make compensation sometimes to get through a round, but in pressure situations, those types of things come out."

The slightest doubt, emotion or hesitation can cause our golf swing to break down. Even a small alteration in a swing can have a rippling effect throughout the body, sending the ball significantly off-target. And there are a number of different ways to choke — physically, mentally and emotionally. Sometimes we choke when we try too hard, or we get too excited or lose control, like Dave Berganio Jr. did in the 2002 Bob Hope Chrysler Classic when he bombed his tee shot too far onto a downslope and lost a playoff to Phil Mickelson.

Here are some effects of over-arousal on your game:

- Your swing becomes too quick, leading to many hazards, including loss of rhythm, failure to make a full shoulder turn and your hands going off target.
- You walk the course too quickly, or your overall tempo is too fast.
- Your swing becomes short, too tight or too tentative, or you quit on your follow-through.
- You tighten your hands on the putter, turning the putter blade so it is not square to the ball or target.
- Your head moves.
- You breathe quickly (sometimes hyperventilating), disrupting the timing and rhythm of the swing.
- If tension limits your breathing, your rib cage lifts and the club does not stay on its plane.
- You lose focus in both shot-making and course management.
- Your putts come up short or often pull to the inside.
- Your confidence wanes, along with your score.

Yikes, It's the Yips

It's bad enough that over-arousal directly affects you and your game, but it has a powerful *indirect* effect, as well. Many golfers learn to become afraid of fear itself. They come to know what effect fear and arousal can have on their nervous system and their swing, so they begin to worry about it ahead of time. They worry about the anxiety they *might* feel and so their fear defence system kicks in before its time has come. Chip Beck, who once shot 59 in Las Vegas and was runner-up in the Masters and the U.S. Open, has had increasing problems with his game in recent years. In the late 1990s, he missed 46 straight cuts, partly through the fear of anxiety, which increased when he was not playing well. "Physically, you start to feel impaired," he said. "You step up, look at your shot and you hit it all over the place. Then it becomes anxiety-driven, and you have a sense of incompetence."

The yips have helped cut short the golf lives of many fine pros, including Ben Hogan, who froze over putts late in his career, and Johnny Miller and Ian Baker-Finch, who both retired to the TV broadcast booth (for the latter, it was because nervousness was taking the fun out of his game).

"A golfer who fears failure — as most amateurs and professionals do, at least some of the time — tends to think about how he takes the club back, how far he turns, how he cocks his wrists, how he starts the downswing, or other swing mechanics," says psychologist Bob Rotella. "Inevitably, he will tend to lose whatever grace and rhythm nature has endowed him with, which leads to inconsistent shotmaking with every club, from the driver to the putter."

Suffering from repeated bouts of choking is often referred to as the "yips." The yips are usually associated with loss of confidence, or shaking or freezing while putting, although they can also rear their ugly head in other aspects of the game.

A study of 1,031 golfers (under 12 handicap) conducted in 2000 by the prestigious Mayo Clinic in Rochester, Minnesota, revealed that more than 25 percent of golfers develop the yips, which adds about 4.7 strokes to the average 18-hole score. Of the golfers who reported experiencing the yips, the average had been playing for 30 years and had experienced the problem for about six years. They were affected most by fast, downhill putts and left-to-right breaking putts from two to five feet. Playing in a tournament or against specific competitors was also associated with episodes of the yips.

The Mayo researchers concluded that the yips may have both physical and psychological causes. Some researchers believe it is closely linked to a disorder called dystonia, which also affects musicians, stenographers, dentists and others who must repeat a prolonged, abnormal posture.

"While pressure situations make the problem worse, it is difficult to imagine why good golfers would suddenly begin having the yips after years of successful performance if it was only a matter of anxiety or choking," said Dr. Aynsley Smith, director of sport psychology and sports medicine research at the Mayo Clinic. "Although performance anxiety may cause the yips in many golfers, muscle and nervous system deterioration caused by prolonged overuse may be at the root of the problem for other players. This may explain why some get relief and play successfully by changing their grip or by switching to a longer putter."

Yet most close observers of the game, particularly golf psychologists, still believe that choking and the yips are mainly psychological. Perhaps we need more studies.

Problems compound themselves when you start trying too hard to overcome the yips, says Rick Todd, golf coach at the University of Texas El Paso. "Dumb mistakes compound more dumb mistakes," he said. "Instead of just relaxing and trying to hit good golf shots, you start trying harder."

Years of anxiety and the pressure of competitive golf can get

---

THE IMPACT OF UNDER-AROUSAL

Under-arousal is probably not as common as over-arousal in competitive golf because it is human nature that competitors have their emergency fear systems activated under pressure, to get "up" for an event. But it happens, as it did to Tom Lehman, who played poorly in the 1999 B.C. Open, partly because he was not motivated and was looking ahead to the upcoming Ryder Cup. "Golf is all about emotion and focus," he said. "And here, I had no emotion. It affected my sharpness and concentration."

When under-arousal does occur, it often has the opposite effect of over-arousal:

- Your swing has no zip.
- You lose clubhead speed and the ball goes off target.
- You loosen your grip and send the putter face off line.
- You can become easily distracted.
- You play too slowly.
- You lose interest in things like a pre-shot routine or lining up a putt.

to you. "The pressure is making me old; it wears me out," said Michael Clark, while competing on the 1999 Nike Tour and frustrated in his attempts to qualify for the PGA.

Tiger Woods agrees: "There are a lot of close tournaments over the years. I can see why many players have grey hair, or they're losing their hair."

EFFECTS OF OPTIMAL AROUSAL

One of the main objectives of this book is to help golfers keep an optimal level of arousal throughout a round. When you don't stay on an even keel, there is a greater chance of your emergency fear system kicking in at unmanageable levels. Optimal arousal will be examined in Sections II through IV, particularly in Section IV. Here are some of its effects:

- Your tempo, rhythm and timing fall into sync.
- You don't think about your swing; you just do it.
- Targets come into sharper focus.
- Your decision-making is better.
- You get 10 to 20 yards more on your drive and generally you need one-half or a full club less on the fairway than you might normally use.
- You score better.
- Your game is fun.

"Most golfers are always just two shots away

from being crazy."

— *golf instructor Fred Shoemaker*

CHAPTER 5

FRUSTRATION:
The Self-fulfilling Prophecy

I f you golf, you know frustration: it's choking on autopilot. Frustration is perhaps the worst kind of choking because it stays in your system for more than one shot.

Psychologists consider frustration a unique type of fear, perhaps the fear of loss of control. We get frustrated or angry because we know darn well what is going to happen next, and we feel we have little control over the outcome. In golf, we may get frustrated with our swing, our opponents, our score or their score, the course or the weather, or a combination of any of these things.

Psychiatrist M. Scott Peck, author of *The Road Less Traveled* and *Golf and the Spirit*, believes frustration is all about narcissism and the strong need for control. "We are inherently narcissistic creatures," he said. "The reason we get angry is that we somehow believe the world should behave the way we want it to. The more strong willed we are, the greater our anger. What extraordinary self-centredness! Our spiritual journey is all about growing out of it." As a golfer, Peck often gets frustrated with his lack of perfection while playing in front of others. "I want to look perfect. I want to be admired. I want it too much."

Frustration can steam-roll a golfer. "When you lose your temper after missing a shot, the chances are you will miss the next shot, too," said Julius Boros, winner of three major championships. Even more grim is the fact that your temper may be just beneath the surface, only a shot or two away in the fickle game of golf. "No matter how well they're playing, a couple of bad shots in a row can change their entire experience," says golf instructor Fred Shoemaker. "They are always on the verge of being upset … I believe the real reason people get upset after a bad shot is that they think they are going to do it again."

We have all probably repeated mistakes and had the helpless feeling of not being able to correct the flaw. During the third round of the 2000 Wegmans Rochester International, the world's best female player at the time, Karrie Webb, looked and acted like a rank amateur, flushed and sulking around the course because her game was off. "I suck," she told reporters, at first refusing to give interviews, then allowing, "I'm very frustrated; usually I play myself out of it. I guess I've got to get over it." This from a woman who had just won four of the previous eight LPGA tournaments!

Jose Maria Olazabal won the 1994 and 1999 Masters, but he became so enraged with a 75 in the opening round of the 1999 U.S. Open, he punched the wall in his hotel room, breaking his hand. Hennie Otto tossed his clubs into a river following a round of 80 in the 2001 South African Masters. And, while blowing away his competitors in the 2000 U.S. Open, Tiger Woods got angry with himself several times, polluting the TV airwaves from Pebble Beach with blue language picked up by microphones on the tee boxes. "In the heat of the moment, I'm one of those guys who plays pretty intense and, unfortunately, I let it slip out. And I regret doing it," Woods said. "I can apologize until I'm blue in the face, but when you're a competitor and you're fighting all day, you can let it go a little bit." Most often, Tiger contains his frustration, but it got the better of him at times in the 2002 British Open when rain and winds pounded him into an 81 to put him out of contention.

Yes, just when we think we have control over the game, it slips out of our fingers. It also happened to Ben Crenshaw of the U.S. in the 1987 Ryder Cup at Muirfield Village. After missing a key putt, Gentle Ben broke the head of his putter and had to finish putting with a one-iron. He lost to Eamonn Darcy, and the European team had its first win on American soil.

Among amateurs, frustration can be epidemic. "My shooting sucked," said Jefferson Glapski, a high handicapper, after a round in Toronto. "A three-putt here, a duff there. A blown tee shot on a par three. Next hole, I nearly hit the damn stop sign after the rest of my foursome — the three stooges — was talking about it as I was driving. Bastards. I began sliding down that slippery slope quicker than Michigan's hopes of winning a Big Ten title. My anger continued to fester." Then Glapski wrapped his five-wood around a tree and part of its shaft impaled his hand and he was covered in blood.

Mike Greenberg, a chiropractor from Atlanta, who has had pro golfer Lee Elder as a patient, complains, "I can't seem to make three pars in a row. And when I mess up, it is difficult to let go of the emotional frustration. Right now, it feels like I'm damned if I do and damned if I don't."

Mount Vesuvius Erupts on the Links

Frustration can spoil our golf game for several holes, for an entire round or it can linger for months. And when it boils over, it can result in profanity, bent clubs, or balls and even clubs tossed into trees and ponds. Sports author and amateur golfer George Plimpton reacted to one of his playing partners throwing his ball into a water hazard by saying, "Of all the indignities that man tries to heap on inanimate objects, throwing a golf ball into the water is perhaps the most hapless. The lake accepts the ball with a slight ripple that disappears almost immediately, leaving the surface smooth, almost smug."

It can be more ominous than that: on occasion, anger has led to "golf rage" on the links. But for most of us, it gets no more sinister than tossing a two-iron down the fairway. "The most exquisitely satisfying act in the world of golf is that of throwing a club," said the late English commentator Henry Longhurst. "The full backswing, the delayed wrist action, the flowing follow-through, followed by that unique whirring sound, reminiscent only of a passing flock of starlings, are without parallel in sport."

In the 1921 British Open, superstar Bobby Jones became upset with the number of hidden bunkers and uneven lies on the fairways at St. Andrews. After just 11 holes, Jones tore up his scorecard and reportedly drove his ball into the River Eden (he later said he regretted this behaviour).

Inability to control temper prevents many golfers from improving, like Tommy Bolt, known more for his antics than his triumph in the 1958 U.S. Open. It was said that "Terrible Tommy" sometimes heaved so many clubs in anger, he nearly emptied his bag. In her younger days, LPGA star Dottie Pepper could fly into a rage. Ky Laffoon, a PGA player of the 1930s, once broke his toe with his putter. Craig Stadler sometimes looks for worms with his wedge. And during the 2000 Senior PGA Championship, Larry Nelson became animated after missing a birdie and bent his putter. He had to use his three-iron the rest of the way.

LPGA Hall of Famer Pat Bradley once grabbed a caddy and screamed at him. On the course, Bradley accused Dale Jones, at that time the caddy for Dale Eggeling, of coughing during her backswing. Jones denied it, but later that day in the scoring tent, Bradley allegedly grabbed Jones by the collar, shook him and shouted, "Don't ever let that happen again!"

Some players believe a short burst of anger can relieve psychological pressure. In the 1996 Rochester International, Lisa Walters became angry over a three-putt and smashed her hand on a portable leader board. "Her hand was bloody, but it broke her anger and she laughed," her caddy, Tom Hanson, recalled. However, Ken Kaisch, a clinical and sports psychologist in Fullerton, California, believes anger is counterproductive. "Psychologists used to think that the expression of anger was good, that it vented or released the pressure inside," he said. "But research is showing that outbursts of anger like those we see on the golf course cause more problems than they solve. The venting actually gets the person more upset. Think about it. You express your anger, which cranks up your arousal level. So you think more obsessively about what happened and you get angrier. Pretty soon, Mount Vesuvius erupts."

Who knows how golf stress can affect your health? Sudden cardiac arrest is the leading cause of death on the golf course, although the age of the victims seems to be more a factor than stress issues, according to Edward A. Palank, a cardiologist in Naples, Florida. Otherwise, studies show that golf has many health benefits, Palank said.

Frustration and over-arousal can distort a golfer's perception of the surrounding activities, thus hurting course management. In scientific terms, the golfer may suffer from tunnel vision, distance distortion, auditory exclusion (tunnel vision of the ears) or denial response (not realizing a serious mistake or violation was committed in the heat of battle).

Society's Pressure Invades the Game

There may be more pressure — and subsequently more choking — than ever before on golf courses. While the game and its slow, firm traditions have not changed, society has. It is generally accepted that society is moving more quickly and people are less patient and less disciplined. "The fact that society's training counteracts that of golf is a problem," Fred Shoemaker says. "The calm and focused state of mind that is necessary for good golf is hard to develop nowadays. We live in a society in which the pursuit of comfort — and the avoidance of discomfort — is deemed a most valuable goal." Combine these factors with an increased number of golfers (especially younger golfers) and you have a climate ripe for more stress and tension.

"Golf is supposed to be this pristine gentleman's game," said Kevin Osborne, an assistant district attorney in Waukesha, Wisconsin. "But it's not much different from the rest of life and society." And in some remote cases, police are summoned to the greens. Osborne investigated the case of 50-year-old Richard Stephens, who died after a case of golf rage on the 18th hole of a course in New Berlin, Wisconsin. According to police reports,

Stephens became angry at comments made by a group of golfers behind him, which included 26-year-old carpet cleaner Tony Osusky. Stephens allegedly took a swing at Osusky and missed. The latter then kicked Stephens who collapsed and died, despite other golfers' attempts to revive him with CPR.

An autopsy revealed that Stephens died of blunt force trauma to the chest and abdomen, and that he may have had a heart condition. No criminal charges were laid after jurors at an inquest decided that Osusky had acted in self-defence.

In 1999, a Cleveland, Ohio, emergency-room nurse, Darrell Cicero, lost an eye when his friend became angry over a muffed tee shot and threw his driver, hitting Cicero in the face and shattering his cheekbone. It happened on the Pine Ridge Golf Course in Wickliffe, Ohio. The accused, 33-year-old bartender/labourer Steve Lacey, pleaded no contest to reckless assault and was fined $500, sentenced to 18 days of house arrest and ordered to perform 100 hours of community service. He was ordered to have anger-management counselling and the judge said he could not play golf for one year. Cicero also filed a civil suit against Lacey.

Slow play is one of the biggest sources of frustration on golf courses, which brings the issue of patience into play. Most of the time, the result is simply a shaking of heads or an exchange of words among the participants. But a course in Washington, D.C., saw a case of golf cart rage in 2000. A foursome, including 55-year-old financial consultant Richard Hutchinson, was putting when two golfers behind them became impatient and shot toward their green. When a ball nearly hit Hutchinson, he whacked it into the woods. One of the men behind then roared toward Hutchinson on his golf cart, but the consultant jumped and kicked with his spikes to knock the man off the cart. "When he was a few feet away from me, I jumped up with my spikes and hit him in his chest and knocked him out of his cart," Hutchinson said. "He was just in a rage." Police took the other man away.

At the David L. Baker Memorial Golf Center in Fountain Valley, California, in 2000, an occasional player in his 20s went berserk. According to police, the man twice shot balls into the group ahead of him, then punched one of the players in the face before running off through a parking lot and jumping a fence. He was later fingered in a police lineup.

All because of golf, they say.

"It's okay to have butterflies in your stomach, as long as you have them flying in formation."

CHAPTER 6

AROUSAL'S GOOD SIDE:
Reaching the Zone

T his great quote on the previous page, attributed to a number of people over the years in sports psychology, suggests that if you channel your emotions, you have a chance for a good performance, even a peak performance of reaching the celebrated *zone*, in which skills and concentration seem to be enhanced.

So far in this book, we have looked at the *negative* altered states of golf arousal. But there is a flip side—arousal occasionally has its advantages. The emergency fear system can be your ally if it is kept running at an optimal level, if your emotions are well managed. Optimal arousal is considered the arousal level at which you feel comfortable while playing golf. Every person's arousal level is slightly different (as you will see in the next chapter). In an optimal state, you are not too aroused or too tense, nor are you too uninterested.

To get some perspective, here are the various degrees of arousal and their symptoms:

- **Over-arousal** — Tension, hyperalertness, anxiety, low energy, freezing, self-doubt, poor awareness, lack of focus, fear of anxiety.
- **Under-arousal** — Sluggishness, lack of drive, lack of focus, boredom, lack of rhythm and tempo, lack of strength.
- **Optimal Arousal** — Extra strength and power, yet relaxed, heightened concentration, dominance, confidence, aggressiveness, increased drive, increased pleasure.

Most players, teachers and golf psychologists say that to reach the zone, a player must achieve optimal arousal for all or part of a round. But reaching that mythical place may be the biggest magic act in all of sports. I'd like to report many cases of golfers being in the zone, and how players are transported to this mystical place, but there don't seem to be as many instances in golf as there are in football, basketball and other sports — and for good reason. After years of researching the subject, I believe that one of the key elements of getting into the zone is an athlete's being able to latch onto an optimal mix of adrenaline, dopamine, endorphins and other hormones released by the mind-body's emergency fear system as an additive to performance under pressure.

But being in the zone is one of the most overworked expressions in sports, and the phenomenon remains largely a mystery and out of our grasp, partly because we can't study it scientifically and partly because we get fooled into oversimplifying it.

In my book *Competitive Fire*, I suggested there are at least four types of zones in sports:

- **Flow** — The romantic version of mind-body harmony in which athletes report such superior concentration and coordination that their task seems effortless. They lose themselves in the action and feel at one with what they're doing. Example: gymnast Nadia Comaneci recording the first perfect 10 in the 1976 Olympics. Over the long haul, flow is probably healthier than other states of mind.

- **The Arousal Zone** — A short spurt of heightened energy, power, speed and concentration during one performance or part of it, often sparked by channelled emotions and hormones. This is flow at an accelerated level, with perceptions possibly more heightened. Call it hyper flow. Example: Michael Jordan getting revenge on a foe who had embarrassed him in the media.

- **The Painless Zone** — A short-term experience in which pain or illness is temporarily numbed but which may result in a mind-body breakdown after the performance. Example: Tom Jenkins shaking off the flu bug to win the 2002 AT&T Senior Open on the Senior PGA Tour. Jenkins believes that adrenaline and endorphins — "my inner troops" — came to his aid.

- **The Long-Term Zone** — This occurs over a stretch of a season or for an entire season or more, often incorporating components from the other three zones as well as momentum and confidence. Example: In 1997, Toronto Blue Jays pitcher Roger Clemens, with a "need to prove" something to the Boston Red Sox (the team that let him go), had his best season in years, winning the Cy Young Award when people said he was washed up.

Although there seems to be a connection among several of these zones, particularly in the altered perceptions of space and time reported by the athletes, we may make the mistake of trying to cram all four into one answer. That may be why we have such a problem getting to the bottom of this subject and why many theories appear to clash. In my research, I would like to report more romance, more instances of the zones. It is true that golf can be receptive to some of these zones of peak performance, but probably not as much as other sports. For instance, fewer cases of the arousal zone have been documented in golf because hormones such as adrenaline and dopamine are more adaptable to physical or explosion sports. Because golf is basically passive, with little chance for physical action and anxiety release, arousal hormones often have a negative impact, resulting in tension and poor play. They crave action, and none comes.

There are not so many cases of the painless zone in golf, because peak health is usually required for long stretches of play (although Byron Nelson said he played best when he was nervous to the point of throwing up the night before an important match, as he did before beating Ben Hogan in an 18-hole playoff in the 1942 Masters. "I always played well when I became sick beforehand," Nelson said.).

Flow

Examples of the flow zone have been reported in golf but they are fleeting, because it is difficult to produce perfect cohesion in a game with such small room for error. Golf is mostly a game of survival and grinding it out, and even the best players report no more than a dozen perfect shots per round. Cases such as Tiger Woods easily winning the 2000 U.S. and British Opens and the 1997 Masters are very rare (even for him), but they do occur.

Greg Norman shot 63 in the 1986 British Open. Nancy Lopez had 64 on the final day to win the 1981 Colgate Dinah Shore Invitational. In 2001, 17-year-old Ty Tryon had 66 in the final round of the PGA Qualifying School to earn his tour card, while in the U.S.

Girls Junior Championships, 17-year-old Christina Kim recorded a 62, the lowest score by a man or woman in USGA championship history. On the LPGA Tour, Annika Sorenstam sometimes gets into such intense focus early in a tournament, you know no one will catch her; that happened when she registered a 59 in the Standard Register Ping event in Phoenix in 2001, the same year Jason Bohn recorded a 58 on the Canadian Tour. And Johnny Miller had 63 on closing day at tough Oakmount near Pittsburgh to win the 1973 U.S. Open in stunning fashion. Miller recalled being very focused, almost in a trance. "Later I saw pictures of my eyes and face and I looked like I was possessed. I looked like I was really in the zone."

In most cases of "in-the-zone" experiences, the golfer has somehow taken control. "I had complete control of my game," said champion Laura Davies after a 66 in the poor weather conditions of the du Maurier Classic of 1996. Remaining calm under pressure was the key for Justin Leonard as he sizzled with a 65 in the final round to capture the 1997 British Open.

Karrie Webb compared her finish in winning the 1999 du Maurier Classic, her first major victory, with an out-of-body experience: "It was like I was watching myself play and make all those good shots ... the last six holes, I was going on adrenaline." She had trailed Laura Davis by five shots on the final day, but was driven partly by criticism from the media that she could not win a major, and shot a sizzling 66.

Webb continues to be fascinated by the zone's mysteries. "When you're in it, you think that nothing can go wrong," she says. "Sometimes it just starts from the first tee. When you hit that first shot in the fairway, it starts things rolling. But golf is a funny game and you never know when it's going to happen, or you're going to make it happen. I guess that what keeps many people intrigued."

Amateur golfer Reg Dunlap of St. Paul, Minnesota, has played just three or four rounds a year for most of his life, scoring between 95 and 100, but in 1986 he played 25 rounds. One day that year, he entered the zone. Dunlap explains, "My drives were long and mostly straight. I started hitting some nice irons, too, and hit some greens in regulation for a change and started picking up pars and tap-in bogeys. It gave me great confidence, but I was also playing in a state of disbelief. I shot 85 on a tough course I had never played. It was a peak experience over four hours, the best fun I've ever had. I have not broken 90 since."

Sometimes a friendly wager can produce the type of optimal pressure a golfer needs to get into the zone. In 2002 at the Glen Ridge Country Club in New Jersey, 23-year-old Eugene Smith went out with five other caddies from the pro shop for a Nassau round of betting. Smith, a 1.7 handicapper, shot 59. Part of his success was probably that he felt at home with his playing partners, but when he plays with golfers of higher calibre, often he has trouble "finding the groove. At the (2001) U.S. Amateur, I didn't qualify for match play. I was thinking, 'Do I belong here?' It was my first national championship and I was having these negative thoughts."

PGA player Jay Delsing said that having fun was the impetus for his 61 at Memphis in 1993. "I just didn't want to run out of holes. I wanted to keep enjoying the day, keep having fun with it. My whole thinking was 'I can't wait to hit it. I can't wait because it's going to be fun.'"

Confidence seemed to be part of the equation in a couple of golfing miracles in Ontario. On September 3, 1997, Gordon Grieve got so pumped up after sinking his first career hole-in-one on the Thunderbird Golf Course in Ashburn, Ontario, that he aced the very next par three, an achievement with odds against it at

64 million to one. Less than three years later at the Oaks of St. George Golf and Country Club near Brantford, Ontario, Oliver Hanratty pulled the same feat.

When pressure is at its peak, near miracles are sometimes reported (although cases of choking are much more common). In the 2001 PGA Championship, Tiger Woods drained two putts from near another time zone late in the second round to avoid missing a cut for the first time in four years. "It was a different kind of situation than I'm used to, and I got a little lucky, but I'm still proud of the way I was able to make those putts," Woods said.

Sometimes two players or more can get into a flow or arousal zone, like Don Pooley and Tom Watson, who battled head to head in an unforgettable duel at the 2002 U.S. Senior Open, forcing one another to produce brilliant shots. Three times Watson drained do-or-die putts, but finally could not beat underdog Pooley.

Mad about Golf

Numerous cases of the arousal zone (or hyper flow) have been reported, especially with anger producing sharpened concentration and brilliant play over a short time, such as with Jack Nicklaus in the 1986 Masters. At age 46, Nicklaus was considered past his prime by many observers, and a column by Tom McCollister in the *Atlanta Journal* suggested he was washed up after winning 17 majors. Nicklaus got angry. "Finished, huh? All washed up, am I? Well, we'll see about that. I really sizzled." Nicklaus pinned the article on his refrigerator door, then went out in a fit of controlled anger, or "cool mad," as Sam Snead often called it, and produced one of the most brilliant victories of all time. His drives were long and accurate, his approaches mostly immaculate and his putting deadly, especially over the back nine when he shot six-under with the pressure at its most intense. "Miraculous" and "stunning" were descriptions Nicklaus used for his play. "I got really pumped up … tears kept coming to my eyes." Besides the media criticism, a large pro-Nicklaus gallery also contributed to his arousal, he said.

Nancy Lopez had a similar experience, partly fuelled by controlled anger, in the 1985 LPGA Championship. Lopez felt she had been unfairly penalized for slow play early in the tournament and focused her anger on her game to win the event. She recalled, "I made anger work to my advantage. I went into tunnel vision. I didn't see the galleries, the TV cameras. I was going to show the LPGA and its officials that I could win in spite of them all. I promise you, nobody could have beaten me that day. I got into a zone where I could see every shot before I hit it, and every shot was perfect in my mind. It was a matter of pride." (The old ego defence again!)

Another time, Lopez got so intense and excited while playing, she said the hairs on her arms and legs stood up (the primitive human's fight-or-flight reaction to a physical threat).

David Ogrin reported a type of precognition while playing in the zone as he shot 26 for the back nine in the pro-am at the 1994 Texas Open. "There was no deliberation, no hesitation, no anguish, no fear, no doubt, no nothing. Everything was crystal clear. The ball was in the air and I could see it bounce before it happened."

In the 1997 Ryder Cup, the underdog Europeans were sparked to an emotional win by fiery team captain Seve Ballesteros, motoring from hole to hole on a golf cart to rally his troops while the home Spanish crowd sang and chanted "Ole!" The Europeans played much better than anticipated and produced an enormous upset.

Tiger Woods knows that pressure and controlled emotions can send his game over the top. "It feels good to be nervous, to have sweaty palms again," he said, prior to winning the 1997 Western Open. "I like being in contention; the pressure gives you a better chance of winning — you feel your nerves, the butterflies going through your stomach."

All of the above reactions and experiences are similar to experiences of other people I have interviewed in non-sports situations over the years: police and emergency services personnel in life and death crises, victims of car crashes and people who have come off the operating table to report so-called out-of-body experiences. We cannot prove that emotions and hormones were responsible, but with so many corresponding anecdotes available, coupled with tests done in university laboratories, they are hard to ignore. They appear to be basic human emotions surfacing while the golfer feels threatened, but he or she is able to funnel them into performance.

Biochemists say that in such cases of controlled arousal, the hormones noradrenaline and dopamine are at work. We'll examine more about controlled anger and how to trigger the correct mix of these hormones in Chapter 21.

PROS IN THE LONG-TERM ZONE

Long-term zones are complex phenomena, involving many factors. Some examples are Byron Nelson's 11 straight PGA Tour victories in 1945; Babe Zaharias' 17 consecutive amateur titles in 1946–47; Mickey Wright's 13 wins, including four straight, in 1963; Lee Trevino's triumphs in the U.S., British and Canadian Opens within a four-week span in 1971; Johnny Miller winning the first three PGA tournaments of 1974 and eight for the season; Nancy Lopez capturing five straight events as an LPGA rookie in 1978; Tiger Woods winning four straight majors in 2000–2001; and Annika Sorenstam capturing four straight events in 2001.

"It just seems to bring out the best in me."

— *Robert Allenby's explanation of his*
7–0 record in professional golf playoffs

CHAPTER 7

DIFFERENCES
AMONG GOLFERS

I f you can relate to some of the stories in this book and not others, welcome to the club.

People's reactions to pressure and fear tend to be highly individualistic, depending on many factors, including the sport they are playing, the situation they are facing, their experience, their gender, their age and their genetic predisposition.

As humans, says Karen Matthews, a professor of psychology at the University of Pittsburgh, our fear defence systems are unique, depending on our nervous hardwiring, our self-esteem, our upbringing and our view of the world. And these things affect the biochemical mix that squirts through our systems when we feel excited or threatened. "Some people are more sensitive than others and are so-called hot reactors, responding up to 30 times a day [to situations]," she said. "Alarm reaction may be an early phase. Depending on your perception of a situation, you have behaviour or response choices to make. If you think there is a threat, your response may be larger."

A study released in 1999 revealed that some people have more cortisol in their systems and may experience more fear than others. And some golfers may be more prone to worrying about their game than others. At the U.S. National Institute of Mental Health, researchers discovered a gene in the human body that regulates a *molecular pump* influencing production of the hormone serotonin, which encourages peaceful thoughts. "If you carry this gene, you may be one of those people who always must worry," says Boston psychiatrist Edward M. Hallowell, a high handicap golfer and author of the books *Worry* and *Connect*, which help people deal with their worries.

Other researchers are learning that arousal is a complex phenomenon and the way people deal with it, or the degree of success they achieve, differs from person to person, golfer to golfer. A study of runners revealed that one in three needed high anxiety before a race in order to run well. "Some athletes perform better under high pressure conditions, whereas others perform poorly," said Robert Weinberg, professor and chair of the physical education and sport studies at Miami University in Ohio. Weinberg says that sport skills that require short, quick bursts of energy and power, such as track and field events, hockey and some skills in football, seem to benefit most from high levels of arousal, whereas precision skills, such as archery, shooting basketball free throws and putting in golf, benefit from lower levels of arousal.

The more average the athlete, the more his or her performance will suffer under pressure, says John D. Curtis, health professor at the University of Wisconsin. "In pressure situations, most athletes tend to get too aroused; that's why they remain average athletes," he said. "They need to relax and let their body and training do their jobs."

Elite athletes, including golfers, can stand increased levels of anger and the feisty hormones it generates when they are performing a task they've been highly trained to do, according to psychologist Charles Spielberger. And different golf shots require different levels of arousal — you should be a little more aroused for a tee shot and a long iron and less aroused for your short game and putting.

Gender Differences

Women and men tend to have different emotional reactions, at least at the amateur level. Men generally have 10 times more testosterone, which promotes aggression and domination, than women. "Testosterone may make men more likely to assert themselves and more likely to strive for a dominant position," says Allan Mazur, a sociologist and professor of public affairs at the Maxwell School at Syracuse (N.Y.) University.

LPGA legend Nancy Lopez recommends that women become more aggressive if they want to shoot low. "The big thing for women, you gotta tell 'em to swing hard," she said. "As in, kill it! Put somebody's name on the ball who you don't like a lot. Just think of somebody. Put their name on the ball, then you just whack it. You're going to play your best golf when you're aggressive."

No one has to tell most LPGA players that. Their aggressiveness and killer instinct rival that of any man. In the 2000 Solheim Cup, Europe's Annika Sorenstam criticized American players Kelly Robbins and Pat Hurst for making her retake a chip because she had breached a minor technicality by shooting out of turn. "It is sad to see that ugly part of them because Pat and Kelly are the nicest they have," Sorenstam said. Robbins apologized, but American captain Pat Bradley stood fast: "When the rules of the game are upheld, the spirit of the game is upheld."

And yet, in my observation of players on the LPGA and PGA Tours, I would say the women tend to be more co-operative with their opponents and a little less competitive than the men. It's not unusual to see defeated opponents stay to congratulate a winner on the green with affectionate displays that do not seem phony. It seems to be the same in amateur golf. "Many women seem more comfortable playing golf with other women, at least in the beginning," says Deborah Longhurst of Brampton, Ontario, co-owner of an interior design company and a high handicapper. "There's not as much competition or as much testosterone flowing as you often see with men."

In general, psychologists say, men tend to be more in touch with their feelings of aggression and arousal because they are exposed to competitive sports from an earlier age than females. Researchers at the University of California, Los Angeles studied another general gender reaction: under stressful situations men tend to be more aggressive while women often gear down through social contact.

The Age Issues

When we talk about pressure and choking and thriving with adrenaline, there seem to be considerable differences among golfers of varying ages.

Consensus is that young golfers who are not into serious competition are less tense and less susceptible to worry. "[Self-doubt] never existed inside my head on youthful summer evenings," says broadcaster Roger Maltbie, a former PGA player. "Rather, the voice I heard as a kid was, 'Wow! You can do this!' Everything was wonderment and imagination. I felt joy playing the game. And it is a game, you know."

In the 2000 Nabisco Championship, an LPGA major, 13-year-old

Aree Song Wongluekiet of Korea stunned the golf world by finishing in a tie for 10th place as an amateur. "I didn't worry about anything; I wasn't that nervous," she said. And yet she did get a little more nervous — and played more poorly — in subsequent tournaments when expectations and pressure were higher. In fact, young players entering serious competition start to suffer and choke through lack of exposure to pressure, according to Derek Gillespie, an all-American at Arizona University, who turned pro in 2000. "Young competitors are more likely to choke," he said. "I don't get as emotional as I did a few years ago. Maturity helps you get over a bad shot." Experience in tough situations helps you deal with pressure, he added. "You get into a situation you've never been in before and you start to tense up."

As competitive golfers age and experience the highs and lows of tournaments, they may change once again. "The older you get, the more fears you get," says veteran LPGA caddy Tom Hanson, who has also caddied on the PGA circuit. "The more mistakes you make, the more fears you have. You see younger players going for the flags because they don't have as many mistakes from the past to worry about." PGA legend Gary Player agrees: "The pressure gets worse the older you get. The hole starts to look the size of a Bayer aspirin."

Johnny Miller said his shank at the 1972 Bing Crosby National Pro-Am stayed with him for years. "It was haunting," he said. "You never forget it. After the Crosby, I never won another tournament without it playing on my mind down the stretch."

"The great players usually start out as confident putters, even bold putters," says golf psychologist Bob Rotella. "But over the years, even the great ones have trouble maintaining this attitude. Maybe playing for years with major championships on the line inevitably produces memories of missed putts in crucial situations.

After a while, those memories become so burdensome that the golfer can't keep them out of his mind as he stands on the green. Then he loses his instinct to look at the hole."

That seemed to happen to Ben Hogan, who was known as the "wee ice mon" for his steely nerves in his younger years, but as he got older, he started to get shaky over putts which helped cut short his brilliant career.

On the other hand, Rotella says that a player's ball-striking may improve with age. "Then it becomes agonizingly apparent that the only thing that is keeping him from winning is his putting. That places enormous pressure that did not exist when he was younger and could blame other flaws in his game for his bad rounds." On the pro circuits, such information becomes public knowledge, Rotella added, "and then the whole world knows he can't make this kind of putt anymore."

Other researchers say that golfers' concentration can improve with age.

One thing for sure, Al Balding of Mississauga, Ontario, didn't allow his creeping age (76) to prevent him from winning the Canadian PGA seniors championship in 2000 as he shot three straight 71s to defeat opponents 20 years his junior. Two years later at age 78, he shot 68 in the same tournament. Balding credited regular exercise, calming techniques and the study of the mental and emotional sides of golf with keeping him on top of his game.

Art Wall Jr. and Sam Snead both won on the PGA Tour after the age of 50. In 2001, Scott Hoch was a two-time PGA winner at 45. In the 2002 British Open, Des Smyth remained in contention into the weekend at age 49.

"Age is just a three-letter word," said Hale Irwin, who contended in the 2001 U.S. Open at age 56.

STRATEGY NO. 2
PRESSURE MANAGEMENT

"Trying to control pressure is my work in progress."
—Rising LPGA star Laura Diaz

In Section I, we looked at the origin of nervousness and how it manifests itself in our mind-body and our swing. Now it's time to start dealing with the issues and the problems, beginning with the subject of pressure and how to keep it at manageable levels so that our emergency fear system does not keep kicking in uncontrollably.

The first important step toward accomplishing this is to develop the mental, physical, emotional and social resources we already have. When we feel too much pressure, it is often because we don't have the resources to deal with it, or they have become depleted.

In Chapter 8, we look at ways to make the physical game of golf a little more manageable as it relates to pressure. Chapter 9 focuses on understanding your goals and the internal pressures you put on yourself, while the following two chapters look at developing confidence and explain healthy worry. In Chapters 12 and 13, we look at how you can ease pressures by developing a type of spirituality and by enjoying things other than the score.

When we keep pressure at manageable (or optimal) levels, we keep our arousal levels at optimal levels. And that is what we are usually looking for in our shotmaking — to be on an even keel, mentally and emotionally. (Showing emotion after the shot is another matter.)

"Don't be too proud to take lessons. I'm not."

— Jack Nicklaus

CHAPTER 8

HOW TO MAKE GOLF
LESS NEUROTIC

E volution has tossed together two unlikely comrades: human beings and golf. We lamented how unnatural golf is to human beings, physically, mentally and emotionally. Alas, in many ways we were not meant for one another. And so, like two people on a blind date, or in the case of some obsessive golfers a blind *wedding*, we must get to know one another quickly. The relationship will take time to grow, but it can. Patience, in this case, is vital. Especially in the beginning, there are steps we can take to make the pairing work.

Above all, your first approach to golf — and the approach you should take every time you lace up the spikes — is one of perspective. You are not playing tiddlywinks here. The standards of the game are abnormally high:

- The goal is to put a tiny ball into a tiny hole hundreds of yards away, using a stick and in just a few shots.
- The rules are rigid and sometimes uptight.

- Even if you play well, bad luck and bad lies happen.
- Things seem set up for you to fail more than to succeed; maybe that's why even the pros call it *survival*.

But there are ways to make the game more user-friendly and less frustrating, less pressure-packed, less frightening. Here are some tips, garnered after interviews with many teachers and players, to help you get off to a good start, or to help you re-load if you want to regain some perspective after your game goes stale:

Buy decent equipment — If you are going to invest time in the game and money in green fees, you might as well give yourself a good chance to succeed. You don't have to spend thousands of dollars or keep changing (or blaming) your clubs; some people in the equipment industry capitalize on our frustration by selling us the newest wedges, balls and other gadgets. Just give yourself a chance for a good start with reasonable equipment.

Take lessons — "All golfers at every level should have a teacher," says PGA player Stephen Ames. LPGA legend Nancy Lopez says the reason many amateurs do not improve past a certain stage is their reluctance to take lessons. Some people might view asking for help as a sign of weakness, but perhaps it is a sign of strength. Golf is a game that should be learned from the ground up, or, in case of sand traps and water hazards, from even further down than that. A few basic instructions can help you diminish the frustrations of trying to hit a little ball with an unwieldy club. Don't worry; there will be lots of room for creativity after you have established your basic, functional swing.

Develop your own swing — Even after only a lesson or two, you can find a swing that is comfortable for you. Don't study the game too mechanically, because there may be no such thing as a "natural swing." At first, practise your swing without using a ball, then introduce a ball but not the pressure. In fact, you should learn to swing with no pressure on you at all, without worrying about where the ball will go.

Forget the score for a while — When you are still learning to play, resist the temptation to keep score. The score can be a huge distraction and a potential source of frustration, which can debilitate learning. It makes the ball look even smaller than it is. To avoid the priority on score, however, you may have to play with others who have the same philosophy, who are not so competitive. Use other barometers to gauge how good a day you've had at the links: the fun, the exercise, the chance to get in the sunshine, the socializing, the escape from home or work. If you conduct business on the golf course, your score should be less important than ever, since it could affect your deal if you demonstrate frustration.

Play alone at first, or with people you don't know — This reduces the pressure and the expectations of people you know, who may bring some personal baggage to the foursome. Familiarity usually breeds a little contempt.

Leave your driver at home for the first year — Sure, the No. 1 wood is a potentially powerful weapon, but remember, we're not at the golf course to impress others with our machismo or prowess. Or are we? The driver is by far the most difficult club to control and often even the pros use a No. 3 wood or an iron off the tee. Eventually you will score with your short game and not so much with your driver, woods and long irons. It may be a good idea for the first year to play almost exclusively at a par three course where you will become closely acquainted with your nine-iron, wedge and putter. If you develop your chipping and putting first, your game will fall into place more appropriately as you proceed.

Choose a golf course that is not beyond your capabilities — Stress and pressure most often occur when we try to do something too challenging for our skill. And never fear the course. Arnold Palmer once said, "Approach the golf course as a friend, not an enemy."

Choose a course with a practice range, or with one nearby — There is nothing more stressful than going to the first tee without having hit a few balls and getting some rhythm and confidence. When you are at the range, stand back awhile and watch others. See how much trouble they have with the golf swing! It's not just you, after all.

Choose a competitive league within your handicap and goals — Just worrying about a Thursday night match can ruin the early part of the week — and your round — if you are worried about keeping up with those golfers who are better than you.

Never fight the golf course — Make a pact with it. Look upon it as a ride on a whitewater raft — don't battle the current, go with the flow. There will be bogeys and double bogeys, but you will survive to gain some pars and the occasional birdie.

Don't overplay the game — Don't overanalyze every shot, don't take too many practice swings and don't overreact, especially to bad shots. Just play the game and keep it a game. Organize a round or a competition in which players are allowed to intentionally distract one another when they are shooting. You might find you can get used to distractions and pressure if you don't always frown upon them.

Don't be so hard on yourself — Once you have come to accept the difficulty of the game, even for professionals who play every day of the year, it will take some of the pressure off you. Lowering your expectations, at least in the beginning, should ease the frustration as you learn. Keep your expectations within reason — don't rush trying to break 100 in the first year or 90 in two or three years. Those goals will come and, chances are, the more you let it happen, the sooner they will come. And give yourself a mulligan once in a while, as long as it doesn't come in a league match or is offensive to your partners.

Be yourself — Unless there is a dress code at the course, wear the clothes you want to wear. Don't worry so much about what people think.

Be physically ready — If your health and energy levels are good, you will tend to play better. Get a good night's sleep before your round and drink plenty of water on the course.

Need a shrink? — Golfers might want to consider seeing a sports psychologist or at least talking to a golf instructor about the mental and emotional issues in their game, especially if they are having a mental block or struggling to get to the next level. It doesn't mean you're crazy (even though you've submitted yourself to a maddening game).

Have fun — *See* Chapter 13.

DEGREES OF DIFFICULTY FOR VARIOUS ACTIVITIES

The following is a speculative look at the degrees of difficulty (with 5 being the most difficult) of various activities. While some people may find the ratings do not apply to them in some instances, I have pieced it together after interviewing many athletes and coaches, and psychologist Robert Weinberg.

Golf played on the course, with others	5
Piano playing without lessons	5
Golf played on the course, alone	4
Tennis and bowling	4
Skiing	4.5
Slo pitch	3.5
Golf on the range	3
Jogging	1
Jogging with a headset	0.5

Practice

If we are serious about the game and want to relieve some of its pressures, we can make inroads simply by becoming better golfers and more confident in our skills. Michigan amateur Dave Greger lowered his scores from an average of 100 to the low 80s in two years "with lots of practice, practice, practice — hitting 300 to 400 balls four to five times a week. There are no shortcuts to better golf."

Too many golfers go to the range and pound away with balls high up on tee or with shots they are good at. But to improve, we should really practise what we are not good at, especially tough shots and recovery shots. These are the ones that can result in embarrassment, doubt or frustration on the golf course.

If we want to overcome the mistakes that make us nervous for the next shot, we must overcome them on the range, says Tom Watson. "The most valuable time to practise is right after your round, when your mistakes are fresh in your mind," he said. "I like to correct a pattern of poor shots as soon as I can. Before the round, I just practise to warm up the engine."

Obviously, the way to get confidence and improve technique in a difficult game like golf is to practise. "A major mistake we make is that we forget how difficult golf is when we don't practise," says Dave Striegel, a sports psychologist at the LGE Sport Science Center in Orlando, Florida. "This is the part that is most illogical about how we sometimes react to poor play. It doesn't take a great deal of practice to improve. The key is to be consistent with the time commitment and to know what to do to address your greatest weaknesses. Making even small improvements in your short game can pay large dividends."

Striegel added players must be realistic and put aside the amount of time they need to practise, according to the level of play they want to reach. "Improving requires being honest about your limitations. If your goal is to see how good you can get, find out what you need to do to get better, reserve some time each week to work on it, then promise to laugh at yourself after each less than perfect shot."

Many players report that they don't feel as much pressure on the driving range. One way to simulate some pressure is to imagine you are playing a hole. If you pretend it is a par five, start with your driver, then hit a fairway wood with your second shot, then a shorter iron for the third. Many ranges have flags at different distances, allowing you some variety with your imaginary holes and shots.

Many fine books offer general suggestions on practice. You might also want to seek out lessons, available at most golf clubs and even practice ranges. Remember that if your goal is to keep lowering your score, your short game and putting will probably require more time than your long game.

Practising your focus and immersing yourself is also valuable at the range, says Debbie Steinbach, a former LPGA touring pro who teaches at The Reserve in Indian Wells, California. She says, "Start by hitting rows of golf balls off tees to free up your swing. Then move the balls down to the grass and feel yourself sweeping each one off the turf. Time will fly by as you bask in the moment. You'll sense an improvement in your rhythm and balance as your swing takes on the feeling of a dance. Forget targets. Your only goal is to get out of your head and into your senses. Feel the club-head at impact. Hear the sound as the club smashes into the back of the ball. See it fly and watch where it lands."

PRESSURE RELIEVER: I HAVE CHOKED

Here's a surefire way to relieve some of the pressure in your golf game: admit that you have choked from time to time. Everybody does, from Annika Sorenstam to Phil Mickelson. Go ahead, don't be afraid to say it out loud: "I choked." You can admit to choking on a shot or for an entire round. There, doesn't that give you some relief? To ease even more of the load, admit that in front of someone else.

But don't confuse choking with being a choker. Just because you succumb to pressure occasionally does not mean you are a choker. So, repeat this aloud: "I am not a choker." Whew, aren't you glad that's over?

"The key to solving the yips, as with many other problems, is to first understand you have them, and then learn how to fix them."

— Dave Pelz, from the Putting Bible

CHAPTER 9

UNDERSTANDING YOUR INTERNAL PRESSURE

If you find yourself standing over the ball and feel too tense or too uncomfortable to take a full swing, join the club. We've probably all felt that way from time to time. But if this is happening too often for your liking, you may want to evaluate what's going on. If the shot is becoming more important than you want it to be, go home at night and face the difficult possibility that the chief cause of pressure in your golf game is *you*, that you are getting in your own way by generating too much internal pressure ... that some of your attitudes, motives and goals may be contributing to your anxiety and choking in golf.

These mindsets — and we all have them to a degree, psychologists say — may include:

- insecurity
- self-doubt
- cockiness
- misplaced desire to prove ourselves through golf

We may be aware of these things and we may not be. They may be conscious, semiconscious (we sort of know, but perhaps don't want to admit it) or subconscious.

Why do you go to the golf course? What do you want from golf? To have fun? To have social contact? To get exercise or enjoy the outdoors? It is unlikely any of these motives is sufficient to produce the internal pressure that may cause you to choke over a shot. If it is an easygoing walk along manicured fairways with easygoing friends, then you likely will not suffer from internally generated tension. Los Angeles cardiologist Arnold Fox, author of several books about stress, advises people in competitive environments such as golf to sit down and write their goals on paper. Let's consider what one or two of your goals might be:

- Play once a week for relaxation, exercise or pure pleasure
- Reduce your score
- Improve to the point where you are competitive with your playing partners
- Hold your own while you are conducting a business deal on the course
- Play with your relatives, or have something in common with your kids
- Join a league
- Win your club championship
- Become a golf teacher
- Become a touring professional

If one of your goals is to become a proficient shot-maker, getting nervous may not be a bad thing. Your emergency fear system can produce arousal hormones, which, if controlled, can help lower your score. But, of course, too much nervousness is generally poison for your game.

Remember that usually nobody does an activity for just one reason, so don't feel guilty if you want to compete as well as to have fun. But don't blow things out of proportion and get frustrated when you have a rocky day on the links, which is going to happen from time to time.

Generally, sports psychologists say, if you are giving too much importance to the shot at your feet, personal issues are probably at work, and perhaps you are not even aware of them. These issues may include self-esteem, the need for status, the need for control or your desire to impress someone. That *someone* may be other people or it may be yourself. You may have set your own standards too high and become nervous when you believe you can't meet them. "Golf provides the perfect opportunity to explore your inner feelings of self-worth, self-acceptance and peace of mind," says Alan Shapiro, a clinical psychologist and founder of Mental Skills Development, an organization offering workshops for amateur and professional golfers. "If you're moody and irritable at home or on the job, you're going to react similarly when things don't go as planned on the golf course. People play golf in a manner not unlike the way they live their lives."

Legendary sportswriter Grantland Rice said that golf "gives you an insight into human nature, your own as well as your opponent's. Eighteen holes of match or medal play will teach you more about your foe than will 18 years of dealing with him across a desk."

A few more questions to consider: Do you go home at night and relive your round in your head? Are you in a negative frame of mind when you score high? On the other hand, do you get too elated with a good round? Think back to your *important* shots of the day. How did you feel just before taking them? Were you consciously aware of your motive for making a good shot? If you can't establish that, be consciously aware of it the next time you play. When you come to an important shot again, stop and think about your motives. Do you hit the ball simply for the sake of pleasure, for seeing it soar into the sky? Or are you trying to impress your partners? Are you trying to get a lower score to look better for your handicap? Are you in some sort of mode to prove yourself? And, of course, how did you feel after your shot? If it is successful, do you feel more powerful, a little more important as a human being? If you hit it poorly, do you feel less of a person? Do you get frustrated? What do you get out of beating someone? How long does the satisfaction last? Does that mindset create more pressure the next time you play?

"When golf performance becomes confused with issues of self-worth and identity, the stakes escalate to the point where it is no longer a game," Shapiro says in his book *Golf's Mental Hazards*.

If personal issues are at work in our game, and we probably all have some to varying degrees, awareness is the first key step if we want to change our course of action and reduce internal pressures. If our pride is too much on the line, we may want to gear back and put more fun into our game. Conversely, if one of our goals is to whittle down our score, an outlook that is too relaxed may hurt us. Establishing what our goals and motives really are can help us reach them more easily. And it can certainly help us to improve, once our psychological baggage is out on the table. Awareness gives us a chance to change our reactions to things.

And change is crucial if our misguided motives are creating pressure when we are trying to shoot a golf ball. Otherwise, we will keep repeating the same golfing mistakes and strategy under pressure, according to psychiatrist and golf consultant Phil Lee. "The greater the pressure, the more likely we are to revert to the old way of thinking," says Lee.

PRESSURE RELIEVER: OTHER COMPETITIONS

It is unrealistic to expect that the mindset of trying to get better (and trying to beat others) will go away in a golf game, when the game is set up for people to be judged. Why not compete for once about who can be the most honest, the most gracious? And once in a while, why not try looking on your partners as cooperators rather than competitors? You will never beat everyone, anyway. There's always someone out there on the course who can score lower than you. What does that prove?

Your Belief and Values System

Once you realize what drives you, you are in a position to make choices about your game. But understand that you come to these choices with baggage from the past — with beliefs and values from the experiences you've had, the upbringing you've been exposed to and even your genetic makeup. These things can affect the way you think about yourself, your motives for playing, even your reaction to pressure situations — in fact, your beliefs and values can *create* pressure as you stand over the golf ball. "Your beliefs play a vital part in all your performances," say British golf instructor Karl Morris and business consultant Harry Alder in their book, *Masterstroke*.

We may be aware of these issues only subconsciously. "The less aware of them you are, the more they are likely to play havoc with the goals you have set," the authors write. "You might say, 'I really want to make a good shot, I really intend to get a better score, I will try my very hardest.' But a belief that says, 'I'm going through a bad spell lately,' or 'There's something not right about this new putter,' will still do its job, acting just like a bunker in your mind."

Alder and Morris, who have consulted with pro golfers such as 1991 Masters champion Ian Woosnam, say that our beliefs and values are at the core of our behaviour on the golf course, also affecting our attitudes and our feelings, but we are often not aware of this complex scenario. They liken this to an iceberg, with only the behaviour showing at the tip, with the feelings a little lower down, the attitudes deeper yet and the beliefs and values at the very bottom and harder to get at. "The underlying beliefs we have about ourselves and our abilities stay below the surface, doing their job very efficiently, but out of sight and out of [conscious] mind. We naturally tend to concentrate on outside behaviour because it is visible and can be analyzed. That is all that a playing partner or coach can see. So it doesn't get our time and attention."

We probably all have some of these mental and emotional issues that have nothing to do with golf and yet they have an important impact on our game: the need to be praised, to be accepted, to overcome self-doubt. Like many touring pros, Allison Finney of the LPGA said she majored in psychology at university so "that you can understand why you're driving yourself crazy."

Some of your motives to be competitive, to beat other people, may come from issues you have not resolved from the past, says clinical psychologist and sports author Robert W. Grant. You may be trying to overcompensate to fill in a type of insecurity, a sort of *emotional hole*, perhaps created from your parenting or childhood, he said. Phil Lee agrees. "We have unresolved conflicts from the past that are activated in the present."

Some of these issues may surface if you worry too much about what may people think if your shot goes awry. One of my main theses is that we choke when we worry about what other people may think about us through our golf game. "I enjoy golf for the social aspects," says Elaine Wood, a high handicapper from Queens, N.Y., "but for the game itself, I'd be better off playing alone because when I start to worry about what my friends think, my swing falls apart. I'm okay on the range, but with other people on the course, my swing seems to be completely different. I feel every arm and leg movement before I hit the ball."

That point cannot be repeated often enough: if you are much better on the practice range than you are on the golf course, you likely worry too much about what others think.

If you are like Elaine, you just stop that right now, or at least adjust your beliefs and values. Don't let others interfere with your enjoyment; rather let them *take part* in it. But first be aware of this mindset. "The desire for others' approval is so basic that most golfers are not even aware of it," says golf teacher Fred Shoemaker. "It is the medium in which they live, much like water for a fish and air for a bird. The fact that this desire is so common as to be unnoticeable makes it even more entrenched in the golfer's mind, and it can easily overpower other commitments that a golfer might try to have."

Are you defending yourself out on the golf course and if so, why? In Chapter 3, we talked about how many people these days defend their egos, but that losing a match or having a high handicap actually is not an attack on your self-esteem. Defence of ego can sometimes result in a sterling performance, but it can also deny us from facing the truth about ourselves and our motives, our goals. And it can inhibit development and learning. The ego may survive in a competitive match, but you may not grow as a golfer and, ultimately, as a person. TV broadcaster Johnny Miller, winner of 24 PGA events, said that PGA great Billy Casper never choked because he kept his ego in check. "If you found yourself playing head to head against him, you were in very deep trouble," Miller said. "He had almost no ego. He would grind along in a very businesslike way, rarely making a mistake, and eventually he would beat you. Remember when Arnold Palmer blew the 1966 U.S. Open to Casper by squandering a seven-stroke lead on the back nine? Well, people forget that Casper shot 32 over the final nine holes."

Ask yourself if it is more important for your playing partners to look upon you as an exceptional golfer or an exceptional human being. Granted, that's a tough question when you are immersed in a golf environment, where too often we are judged by how few strokes we can get around in. We live in a society where competition is important, where being number one is the ultimate high. If you could get inside other people's heads, you would probably find they don't think any less of you as a person because you dribble the ball off the tee once in a while, or even if your overall game stinks. But they likely think less of you if you keep losing your temper, disrupting their game by constantly complaining or trying to keep your score down through cheating.

If you are hell-bent on impressing, why not do it by building a fancy home or a stunning resumé? Check your vanity at the clubhouse. Unless you are preparing to become a pro or the club champion, consider the golf course as a place to relax, to escape the rat race. But, if you continue to look upon the golf course as a proving ground, there are fewer places with lower frustration levels. Anyway, who are we trying to prove things to — our parents? Siblings? Ourselves?

Psychologists suggest making the expectations you live up to yours and yours alone. This is one major reason why Tiger Woods is head and shoulders above the pack in the PGA. He has stopped living and playing for others. "I've always been a big believer of you having your own goals, your own expectations," he said. "Go live for those."

Self-expectations, though, must be kept in perspective. LPGA legend Pat Bradley said she stopped improving when she tried too hard. "One of the best pieces of advice I have ever received is to go easy on myself," she said. "I was always very, very hard on myself and I did not accept mediocre. I had to lighten up on myself and pat myself on the back a little bit more and embrace the moment rather than fear the moment."

All of this, of course, is the kind of stuff that may not sink in until you get home from the course. Sometimes in the middle of heated competition, with your adrenaline flowing, it is easy to get caught up in the proving game. And yet it is possible to worry less about what others think. Success has been reported by Birlie Bourgeois, a petroleum engineer in Houston, Texas, who was frustrated by how his scores were rising from the mid-80s into the 90s. After reading my psychology column on the internet, he suspected part of his problem was what others thought of his game. When he became aware of it, he started playing more for himself. "I kept it in my mind that no one was watching me but me, and that it's just all fun. I actually was smiling (during a round) and it was a great tension reliever. I even saw results from my fancy-free attitude on the putting green. I was awesome. I turned that nervous energy into positive focus and, wow, you were right, everything changes."

Changing Your Course

Let's say you are having problems with pressure. You examine your psyche (maybe even get down as far as your beliefs and values) and determine that you don't like enough of what you see. But it makes you feel uncomfortable. "Many golfers don't understand how the mind works and feel more comfortable working on their swing rather than their attitude," says golf psychologist Patrick J. Cohn.

WHAT YOU THINK OF YOURSELF

What you think of yourself and your golf game is also very important. Many people are too critical of themselves, leading to constant choking or at least to underachieving, sports psychologists say. And all human beings show insecurities from time to time, says psychologist Alan Shapiro. "None of us are so godly as to be entirely self-assured and comfortable with who we are."

"No real progress in golf can be made without an honest acknowledgment of the inner obstacles that human beings put in the way of themselves and the expression of their potentialities," writes author W. Timothy Gallwey in *The Inner Game of Golf.* "Whereas there is a more widespread belief in human potential than there used to be, it seems as hard as ever for most of us to own up to our tendency to get in our own way. And when we do acknowledge it, we tend to be so hard on ourselves that we become helpless to do much about it. Only if we find the courage and honesty to admit to our own self-interference and become more alert to it as it arises will we be able to make effective use of the plentiful technical information available."

Some golfers may even feel shame when they don't perform properly. "When you play well, you feel self-assured, one of the gang,"

It *is* hard to change. It will not be easy to make adjustments but you may have more control over your future than you think, especially if these changes are not major ones. Chances are, you've made changes in some areas of your life — you've been able to shift priorities at home or work and become less materialistic or less goal-oriented. It may be just a matter of transferring that to the golf course, of getting your priorities in order on the links.

Shapiro said. "On those days when your game is off, you experience the isolating emotion of shame, which immediately cuts the ties that connect you to the rest of the world. Shame is an extremely powerful emotion in that the manner in which you experienced it as a child could potentially stay with you throughout your entire life. What changes is that as an adult, you have internalized the harsh, critical voice of your parents. It is now you shouting and continually reminding yourself that 'You deserve to be ashamed!' ... but you are no longer a child and you do have the power to change your thinking patterns, to formulate your own self-evaluations."

Gallwey says that constant self-criticism causes self-doubt over the golf ball, and that you must make a distinction between yourself and the voice of doubt inside your head. "When doubt knocks at your door, no one says you have to open it," he said. "However, if, like me, you were raised in an environment of doubt and always having to prove yourself, it's possible to become so enmeshed in it that you can't tell the difference between yourself and the doubt."

Psychiatrist M. Scott Peck says we must learn emotional "detachment" from the issues and psyches which are giving us problems. In his book *Golf and the Spirit*, he offers a three-step process to this detachment:

- **Self-diagnosis** — Realize you have a problem and name it. On occasion, you may need to seek the services of a professional (golf pro or psychotherapist) for assistance in finding the right name for your disorder.
- **Kenosis** — Having named the problem, get rid of it. Empty your emotional investment in your old pattern. You have to want to do it so badly that you are willing to surrender those old attachments.
- **Practice** — Empty yourself of the destructive detachment, again and again. A neurosis is not like a little pebble you just kick off to the side of the road — it is a boulder you must chisel away at day after day, month after month, year after year.

That is pretty heavy stuff. If you are having a hard time doing this, why not start by trying something corny, such as giving yourself a different name on the golf course, perhaps a nickname. Or change your signature in the clubhouse. Now that's detachment! Do something to change your first tee habit and see if it eventually eases the pressure on your game, or eases the pressure on your internal motives.

Change takes discipline, but isn't that what golf is largely about? Author Tim Gallwey came to a point in his golfing life where he wanted to play "with less ego interference" and, with discipline, he pulled it off.

Joe Inman decided to change his thinking in the middle of the Bell Pacific Senior Open of 1999, and it was a case of choking under pressure that prompted his turnaround. Near the end of the final round, Inman held a three-stroke lead over the field when suddenly a noise distracted his concentration. He recalls, "Some kid in a tent near the 18th hole let out a yell. My brain exploded and my shot went into the water. I went from feeling in control to my world crashing down around me." But it suddenly occurred to Inman that his priorities were askew if his entire world, his ego, revolved around a golf shot. "I said to myself, 'Joe, be a man, son … this is just not that important. This is not life and death.'" As soon as he said that to himself, his composure returned and he went on to win the tournament. And he was more content with himself in future tournaments. "I have much more peace inside," he said. "Your legacy should be your children and friends, not your trophies. I don't want to be the richest guy in the cemetery."

"I can't seem to get my confidence back. It's really affecting my nerves and my swing. Do you have any suggestions?"

— Three-time LPGA winner Lisa Walters

CHAPTER 10

THE CONFIDENCE
WE SHOULD HAVE

The scenario would shake the boots off most mortals. A lifetime high handicapper, age 67, was ready to tee off in a foursome that included the world's greatest player and perhaps its most famous athlete — Tiger Woods — at seven o'clock on a late summer's morning at the Royal Montreal Golf Club. About 2,000 people, including representatives from most of the major daily newspapers, TV stations and media organizations across Canada, were assembled. With the eyes of the world upon him, the aging hacker, whose game was rusty from inactivity, stepped up and belted the ball 175 yards up the middle. The crowd, having feared he might dribble the ball a few yards, erupted into hearty applause.

The man was Canadian Prime Minister Jean Chrétien and the only thing he had going for him at that moment was his confidence under the gun. "Even in heated debates in the House of Commons, I had never felt such pressure," Chrétien later admitted. But he proved that misty morning in the pro-am for the 2001

Bell Canadian Open that confidence can win the day for you (or at least the moment; the rusty Chrétien went on to shoot 100).

Yes, we have discussed at length what a force ego can be in our game. It may now sound ironic — and isn't golf wrapped in paradoxes? — that many, if not all, golfers who have big egos sometimes suffer from lack of confidence. Without confidence in golf, there is no point hauling the clubs out of the trunk of the car. Without confidence, you don't trust your swing to be smooth, or your putts continually fall short. Without confidence, your emergency fear system gets out of hand and you choke.

However, *with* confidence, you don't let negative thoughts interfere with your swing and you don't worry about missed shots because you know you are going to make a lot of them. With confidence, Jean Chrétien can retain that funny little smile on the side of his face. Said Sandra Palmer, a 19-time LPGA winner, "There are people better coordinated than I am and with more ability, but if I had to choose, I'd take somebody with confidence over somebody with natural talent." With confidence, some golfers have willed their way to victory, or to a lower score.

We can look at confidence in two ways:

- It is something you acquire after practising hard, getting your game down and performing well over the course of time.
- It is a mindset you can encourage and develop, even without a stunning resumé.

After decades of coaching amateur sports and interviewing elite athletes, I believe both definitions are true. For most of my life, I believed the first definition was by far the strongest, but the more I delve into human achievement, the more I believe the second definition *can* be influential. In fact, we have no option but to choose the second if we want to come close to reaching our potential. The human psyche just has too many self-doubts, negativities and weaknesses to wait and hope that all the pieces will fall into place and we will suddenly wake up one morning with confidence.

Yes, patience remains a virtue and so does hard work, but we must also work hard in the psychological realm. You cannot wait too long for some things and confidence is one of them. "You have to train your mind for success," said PGA player Calvin Peete. "When I first joined the tour, I didn't think I was as good as I was. Now my mental has caught up with my physical."

Because we have thought of confidence for so long by definition number one, the word has become too stereotyped. It is altogether too soft and ambiguous. Confidence sounds like something that just happens to wash over us. "Positive thinking" is another mushy term. Just think good things, people tell you, and you will succeed. I also believe that to be partly true, but it's not aggressive enough to take hold as a solid mindset. Rather, let's use the term "proactive." There's more action involved, and you must take action to get to the level of real confidence. Positive thinkers believe things will turn out peachy. Proactive thinkers believe things will turn out well, but they will also help make sure it happens.

Thinking big is a crucial part of proactive thinking, especially if you want to become an elite golfer, according to psychologist Bob Rotella. "Champions all have a few common characteristics. They are all strong-willed, they all have dreams and they all make a long-term commitment to pursue those dreams," he said. "On the other hand, a player with no dreams has little real potential." Rotella doesn't think of himself as a "shrink" but as an "enlarger" who believes in people's high hopes and abilities.

Confidence and Self-Esteem

When discussing the complex human psyche, we should differentiate between confidence and self-esteem. Self-esteem is the bigger picture. It's what you think about yourself. You can have good self-esteem and yet suffer from bouts of waning confidence, especially in a fragile activity like golf. And yet many golfers have shaky self-esteem.

"Golf is such a difficult game — albeit one that can be mastered — that many golfers suffer from terrible self-esteem," says two-time U.S. Open winner Hale Irwin. "When a golfer who regularly shoots in the mid-80s is asked what he shoots, he usually says low 80s. It's not that he has such a good impression of himself, or that he's a flat-out fibber. It's that he has low self-esteem because he shoots in the mid-80s — even though that's a perfectly good score for a great number of golfers."

The problem, according to Irwin, is that many golfers see their glass as half empty. "The half-full golfers — a fraternity to which I belong — are constantly striving for more, reaching for the stars. The half-empty guys are looking for a place to wreck. People who have this attitude are prohibiting themselves from moving up the ladder ... but the best thing confidence does is breeds more confidence. It makes you feel better and think better and execute better."

Even the world's best can suffer from lack of confidence. "I'm just getting confident being on the leader board again," said Annika Sorenstam in the 1999 New Albany (Ohio) Golf Classic.

And this from a woman who had previously won 17 tournaments and nearly $5 million in career LPGA earnings! Golfers are more susceptible to self-doubt and choking, Sorenstam said, when they are in a streak of not playing well, when something is off with their swing. "You start to ask yourself why you are not playing well and it starts to wear on you."

And this from Meg Mallon during the 2000 Wegmans Rochester International: "I hope the person [herself] that showed up today shows up for the next two days." Mallon went into that event with 11 LPGA victories. Her prayers were answered and she came from behind to defeat Dale Eggeling.

What separates most golf pros from the rest of us (besides the time they spend on the game) is that their self-esteem, or at least their golf esteem, is strong enough that it keeps them in contention week after week. It is solid enough to survive occasional drops in confidence. "My confidence in my game is what drives me," Sorenstam says. Greg Norman is as much known for his defeats in major tournaments as for his 71 career victories, but he said after failing to capture one tournament, "I am a winner. I just didn't win today."

Jeff Maggert captured a PGA tournament in 1993, then went six years without winning while finishing second a dozen times. He admitted to losing confidence and choking occasionally, "but I knew in my heart eventually I was going to win another tournament." He did — the Andersen Consulting Match Play World Golf Championship in 1999, beating Tiger Woods along the way. "To talk to the press was almost like a tape recording," he said. "I knew what I was going to say before I even came in." Added Maggert, "You have to approach every day with a lot of enthusiasm and a lot of confidence in your game."

"That sense of supreme confidence serves athletes well," says Andrew Lovy, chairman of the psychiatric department at Columbia Olympia Fields Osteopathic Hospital in Olympia Fields, Illinois. "Once athletes have that confidence, they don't feel the pressure of the game. They consider that this is the epitome of what they've practised for. This is the reason they've developed their skills ... the physical mastery of a skill, the practice, comes first. Without that, it's all desire. And there are a lot of wannabes out there who haven't paid their dues."

Preparation is a key to keeping doubts at bay, says Marlene Streit, named Canada's amateur female golfer of the 20th century by the Royal Canadian Golf Association. "It mainly comes from being well prepared for a tournament or a particular shot," she said. "Look at how confident Tiger Woods is, even after he makes a couple of bogeys; that's because he's so well prepared." Streit added, however, that confidence can be a fleeting thing. "You can hit a couple of bad shots and start to doubt your swing." A lot of confidence comes from familiarity of playing the same course, she added. "Some players are great at home where they feel comfortable with the course, but not so good when they have to travel."

"Every time I play, in my own mind I'm the favourite," says Tiger Woods. "I personally believe in myself and my abilities. I've seen myself do it time and time again, not necessarily in tournaments, but even when I'm out practising or out on the golf course by myself. I'll throw a few balls down and shape the shot the way I want to. If I can do it there, I can definitely do it in a tournament. You take that belief into a tournament and you're able to kind of build on it. Under pressure, you win with your mind. And the earlier you can do it in your career, the easier it is to repeat it."

Babe Didrickson reportedly once said to her opponents prior to a tournament, "I don't know why you're practising so hard to finish second." (Overconfidence on the golf course is another matter entirely, especially when you underestimate the course or your opponents.)

Whenever a golfer moves up a level, whether it is after breaking 100 or 90 or finally moving into a club championship, the ticklish issue of confidence often comes into play. Diana D'Alessio had that situation in her rookie 2000 season on the LPGA Tour when she said, "It's a battle for me out on the course. I'm fighting two forces. Part of me has doubts and the other is very confident. I'm trying to make the self-confident one win."

This pecking order exists at a higher level. In the 1970s, Tom Watson was one of the world's best golfers, but he was known for cracking under pressure, partly because he was intimidated by an even greater golfer, Jack Nicklaus. It wasn't until he defeated Nicklaus for his second British Open title in 1977 that Watson said he felt he belonged in such elite company.

It can add to our confidence if we know that our opponents have occasional self-doubts. Nicklaus was ahead of his time in recognizing this psyche. "In the majors, you knew when it got closer to the final day, the pack ahead of you would fall back because of the pressure," said Nicklaus, who outlasted his opponents when the going got tough in the important events. Statistics back him up. From 1960 through 1980, Nicklaus played in 289 non-major events and won 50, for a 17.3 winning percentage. In the four majors, the Masters, the PGA Championship and the U.S. and British Opens, despite playing against more talented fields, Nicklaus won 17 of 76 events for a 22.4 percentage (he won the 1986 Masters when he was out of his prime).

Summoning Our Resources

I believe everyone is capable of some sort of greatness. Sadly, most people don't achieve that for a number of reasons, including lack of opportunity or support from those around them. But we can control our destiny more than we think, and it all starts with thinking we can. Don't listen to other people's criticism and cynicism. They have their own reasons for not succeeding and many would like to pull you down with them. Make a pact with yourself now: I will not be afraid of what others think. If I am going to fail, I will do it without their help!

You have a lot of things going for you. Stand in front of the mirror and look at yourself. Even if you are out of shape, your body was built for action, and your mind is potentially more effective than any computer. You are born with hand-eye coordination, flexibility, survivability, strength and stamina. Try putting a price tag on your potential ability. You can't. We are walking miracles. We have every right to be confident with almost anything we prepare ourselves for.

CONFIDENCE AS AN EMOTION

Most golfers might not see confidence as an emotion, but I believe it can be. We don't give confidence enough credit because it is not as clearly defined as other emotions such as anger or joy. But if confidence is not a full-blown emotion, it is at least a link between emotion and reason. We get into a confident state of mind because we have shot well in the past, and so we get the adrenaline, the dopamine and the endorphins going in the right direction.

THE GOLFER AS WARRIOR

If you are a serious competitor golfer, or want to become one, you may want to go a little beyond the confidence or proactive state.

When a golfer feels like a kind of warrior and develops a feeling of dominance over a foe or a game, the powerful emergency fear system, the product of millions of years of warfare and survival, can kick in with its hormones, such as dopamine and testosterone, pumping out in buckets. These hormones, of course, are often hard to handle and can make a golfer irritable or angry, so it is with delicacy that I bring up this subject in what is generally a gentle game of golf.

The greats look upon themselves as warriors going into battle, such as the teams for Europe and the U.S. in the Ryder Cup. Even the usually staid Tom Lehman pumps his fists, Justin Leonard leaps into the air and the Europeans often play beyond their expectations. "To win a Ryder Cup in the States is unbelievable. It took courage and guts," Tiger Woods said as his team battled in the 1999 event in Brookline, Massachusetts. Little wonder the Americans fought back from a four-point deficit to triumph. They had a motivational meeting the night before the final matches, complete with inspirational messages from other athletes and a poem by Alamo soldier William Barrett Travis — read to them by presidential candidate George W. Bush — about fighting until the end. Two years earlier in Spain, it was Europe's Seve Ballasteros who delivered the rallying cry. Individual golfers have carried tough-minded play into battle, even nice guys such as Nick Price, Ernie Els and Nancy Lopez.

Sometimes these warrior mindsets have a biographical base. Lloyd Mangrum was awarded two Purple Hearts after being wounded twice in the Battle of the Bulge in World War II. In the 1946 U.S. Open, Mangrum battled to a playoff win over Vic Ghezzi and Byron Nelson, a cigarette dangling dramatically from his lips. And sometimes the golfer has always wanted to be a real warrior, like Greg Norman, who as a boy in Australia dreamed of becoming a fighter pilot.

While battling personal demons in the form of an alcohol problem, Notah Begay III triumphed for two PGA victories in both 1999 and 2000. In his amateur career, Begay (a Native American) used to put two dabs of ceremonial red clay on his cheeks before an important golf match in what his opponents referred to as war paint. "That custom is a bit of a distraction now," he said in 1999. "But I still see every single round of golf as a long journey. You never know where you're going to go and you don't know how hard it's going to be."

Tiger Woods, who can bench-press more than 300 pounds in early-morning workouts, believes his aggressiveness and sometimes emotional play are part of a type of warrior mentality. "Once I get going, I tend to keep it going," he said. "And maybe that's just because how emotional I am when I play. I get fired up and I enjoy it." On Sundays, Woods often wears red, the colour of bullfighting, of boldness.

Karrie Webb embraces battle. "Of course, you get butterflies in your stomach and the adrenaline runs through your body," she said. "But I love that feeling. I'm not scared in those situations."

(Although there are times for dominance and aggressiveness among highly competitive golfers, generally they seek a peace of mind, an inner calm for their overall game, knowing that a temptation to always play on high adrenaline can be fatal. Woods is a prime example, visiting a Buddhist temple once a year with his mother. He draws on some of its philosophies and mental powers to help his game.)

Besides confidence, another cliché in competitive golf is courage. Real courage is feeling afraid and going ahead with the battle, anyway. If fear of others is the prime cause of tension and choking, then real courage is forging ahead with a tough shot, even though people might think less of you if you fail. Annika Sorenstam has wavered in the pressure of many major tournaments, but for the final round of the 2001 Nabisco Championship, she wrote a note to herself in her native Swedish where she could see it on her visor: "Don't be afraid. Just go for it." I think that's what all super-golfers have. They are not afraid to take a chance under pressure, even though they might end up looking foolish in some people's eyes. Bear with me on this one, but I believe that if Sorenstam, Woods and Nicklaus are afraid of anything, it is of being seen as too wimpy to take the chance under fire. If they take that chance, it doesn't matter if they succeed; they've already beaten their demons.

You don't have to be playing for a green jacket or a club championship to show a warrior's courage. Facing your own fears — indeed, your own weaknesses and needs — may be the biggest test of all.

CHAPTER 11

HEALTHY WORRY:
The Emotional Drive of Our Game

When I wrote a psychology column for golf.com in 2000–2001, I received many queries from golfers around the world, asking for advice about the mental and emotional aspects of their game, and also about worrying. They worry about lots of things:

- **Patrick Falvey**: "I have a terrible chipping problem. All other parts of my game are strong, but it is starting to affect my whole confidence and appetite for the game."
- **Thom Geishauser**: "I put too much pressure on myself."
- **John Dunbar**: "I conquer my fears with alcohol and I'd like to find other means."
- **Susan Farron**: "I have been a pro on the European and Futures tours for five years. The last two years have been a huge struggle with my confidence ... I have completely lost my eagerness to even go to the golf course."

- **Y. P. Das**: "I have a problem eliminating bad swing thoughts from my mind."

These problems are bad enough when they are confined to the golf course, but many golfers tell me they take their issues home and worry about them. And this long-term worry compounds the situation once they get back to the course. Caroline Wright, who is trying to become a serious golfer in the Los Angeles area, says she sometimes goes home after a round — even a good round — and performs what she calls a "mental autopsy" on the 18 holes. "Mostly I cringe and linger over the missed shots, the ones which missed the green. In my mind, I shoot them over and over. Some nights, I can't seem to get past this. I think sometimes my husband wants to leave me. He's not a golf widower. I think it's worse."

Worry, of course, can lead to tension and irritability, even depression, and can make life uncomfortable for those around us. If it continues, worry is called *vigilance* and the hormones it drips into your system, including cortisol, can cause illness. An early researcher in worry, Dr. Charles May of the Mayo Clinic, said that worry "affects circulation, the glands, the whole nervous system, and profoundly affects the heart. I have never known a man who died from overwork, but many who died from doubt."

That may be a little extreme for a game of golf, but remember from this book's introduction the quote from Ron Gropp, a seven-handicapper from Toronto who was concerned over his game to the point that, "I have cried many times over this." This is our worry system at work, the first cousin of the emergency fear system, as described in Chapter 2. But, of course, worry has its benefits.

Simply thinking too much about golf between rounds or

between tournaments has hurt two-time U.S. Open winner Lee Janzen. "It can serve you well over the short term, thinking about what you have to do in a round the next day," he said. "But I get exhausted thinking about strategy. It can wipe me out for two weeks after a tournament."

For amateurs, fretting about your golf game may not kill you, but it will undoubtedly take away from your enjoyment.

SUPERSTITIONS

Many golfers engage in quirky superstitions or rituals to try to get mental control of a difficult, fearful game.

Jack Nicklaus keeps three coins in his pocket while playing. Davis Love III marks his ball only with a 1965 or 1966 penny, while Lorie Kane uses a lucky Canadian loonie and Jesper Parnevik never marks his ball with the coin "heads up." Karrie Webb shaves her legs on the first day of every tournament, "whether I need to or not."

Such behaviour, psychologists say, is geared toward keeping the golfer centred in a routine that stays the same day after day, or win after win.

It's also an attempt to keep control in a stressful situation, says sports psychologist Tom Saunders, author of *Golf, the Mind-Body Connection*. "If you believe in something very strongly, it will happen. It's the placebo effect," he said.

But sometimes superstitions backfire. Psychologist Merry Miller says that if a golfer sleeps in on the day of a tournament and rushes to the tee without warming up, then shoots a good score, she might think this routine is needed all the time. "She's attributing her performance to this behaviour, but this is not healthy behaviour," Miller said.

The Worry Busters: Awareness and Action

So how do we avoid these *mental autopsies* that agonize people such as Caroline Wright? Psychiatrist/amateur golfer Edward M. Hallowell recommends that golfers who worry too much release it with regular exercise, meditation or music, or by *worrying in pairs* with other golfers who have similar issues. Before that, however, Hallowell says we must recognize that we are worrying, and that is not always obvious. In fact, most people probably have no idea that the average person has 66,000 thoughts a day, two-thirds of them negative. Hallowell and other experts believe that, in general, this is nature's way of motivating us, a type of survival mechanism. "It's a sort of fear, and we all know how motivating fear can be to the human species," he said. But there are *healthy* fears and *unhealthy* fears, Hallowell added, "and unfortunately, the majority of people have more unhealthy fears than healthy ones."

An example of a healthy fear in golf is when you have an important match in a week's time on a course with long par-five holes. Your woods are not up to snuff, so you go to the range and work on them. An example of an unhealthy fear is worrying that if you lose next week's match, your opponents will think less of you. (If they do, then they are battling with their own unhealthy fears.)

When we feel worried or anxious about an upcoming situation, whether it's a league match or a business deal on the links, the most important thing is awareness that it is a type of fear. Without awareness, we can't proceed to the next steps. We must become aware that our worries may be needless (unhealthy) fears.

Emotional Drive

Worry and insecurity are most often hazardous to our golf swing. That is one of the main thrusts of this book. Yet healthy worry

PRESSURE RELIEVER: DEAL WITH WORRY

Here are some tips on dealing with worry, put together after interviewing several psychologists and psychiatrists. If you are worrying about something, you must:

- Recognize it as a fear (that may be the one big admission to face) and identify where the fear comes from; it may be a fear of failure or a fear of what others think.
- Separate healthy fears from unhealthy fears; most fears are unhealthy and don't have a realistic chance of occurring. Healthy fears, involving things we have some control over, can help you thrive in a threatening situation, or even just solve a problem.
- Take action; worry is action thrust into reverse gear.
- Defuse as soon as possible unhealthy fears by changing your mindset. The use of relaxation techniques and humour are valuable.
- Redirect healthy fears into preparation or action; you must look on a situation as a challenge, not a worry.
- Concentrate on the solution, not the problem.
- Recognize that you have control; remember that, in general terms, life is 20 percent what happens to you and 80 percent how you react (some may argue that in golf, the percentages are reversed).

can be a big power boost to our game over the long run.

Psychologists say that worry is a type of fear, a long-term one rather than an immediate fear. We worry about how our golf game is progressing or about the game tomorrow and who we might play with. We may even worry if we will top the ball on the first tee. Worry is good for our competitive golf if we use it to improve our weaknesses. But it is bad if it dominates and ruins our enjoyment.

After much research into the subject, I refer to worry as the *bogeyman force*. That's not bogey, as in the golf boo-boo, but bogey as in an unseen potential problem. It is not so bad to have a bogeyman in the next country, a day or so away. That's how we can categorize our long-term "healthy" worry to improve competitively. But a bogeyman under our bed is another matter. If the worry is that close — on the day of the match — can sabotage our swing. The bogeyman under the bed is the reason so many golfers choke during a match.

The better golfers recognize healthy fear and use it to progress. They use its energy — I call this *emotional drive* — to practise, to learn, to plan. If used properly, emotional drive is an elaborate survival defence, a cousin to our immediate-response defence, the emergency fear system. In humans, emotional drive is much more developed than it is in animals, although some animals also have long-term defences with their social networks, lairs and migratory patterns. If defend, defend and defend some more seem prevalent in this book, it is what survival in competition is all about, whether physical, social or athletic survival. And, of course, we know all about the defence of our ego (*see* Chapter 3).

The bogeyman is an insecurity that can create long-term pressure in a golfer, and even healthy worry. "Pressure is a blessing for those who know how to control it," says golf psychologist Patrick J. Cohn. "Pressure increases your motivation to practise, boosts your concentration to help you hit a difficult shot and supplies extra energy. Pressure becomes a problem only when you don't cope with it and it takes you out of your optimal emotional zone."

Some great players watch their bogeyman get out of shape and less scary over the years. Karrie Webb told me in 2002 that in the preceding 12 months, she had lost a bit of her motivational edge, "because I reached and went beyond my dreams so early in my career. I've had to reset my goals again to get motivated." Of course, during 2001 and 2002, Annika Sorenstam's own bogeyman was at work; she was highly motivated to wrestle the number one ranking away from Webb and she did. That is, until the 2002 Women's British Open when a newly charged Webb defeated her.

Where Was the Bogeyman Born?

Many psychologists believe that such worry is a key component in a successful person's drive, whether in business, politics or golf. This is a complicated subject with many variables and issues, but high achievers are often driven to achievement, at least partly to prove something to somebody, perhaps to themselves, and they are never satisfied, despite considerable trophies. (Remember Jack Nicklaus' statement about embarrassment being his number one motivator?)

Superachievers often seek to fill an "emotional hole" through their work, and this becomes a type of overcompensation. Many golfers say they got into a mode where they wanted to prove themselves to others, especially when they were younger. Beth Daniel was the LPGA's rookie of the year in 1979, partly, she said, "because I had the attitude that I'm Beth Daniel and I belong out here, and I'm going to prove it. Golf was a matter of life and death then."

All-time great Gary Player isn't sure where his drive comes from, but he acknowledges how strong it is. "What I have learned about myself is that I am an animal when it comes to achievement and wanting success. There is never enough success for me."

Sometimes the bogeyman seems born out of poverty and the early physical needs of many professional athletes. As a golf psychologist to many pros, Dick Coop, a professor of educational psychology at the University of North Carolina, has seen the power of insecurity. He says, "The linkage of fear, insecurity and motivation is often mentioned in discussions of golf greats such as Ben Hogan, Sam Snead and Byron Nelson. Lesser golfers felt the same fear. With these older golfers, much of the fear stemmed from their humble beginnings in life. Hogan sold newspapers on street corners and spent time in the same caddy yard as Nelson. Their insecurity is understandable: they knew how tough life could be for them if they failed to produce on the course. There were fewer options if they didn't succeed at golf, because most of them didn't have a college education to fall back on, as is the case with today's generation of tour golfers. In many ways, a secure tour player is a foolish tour player. If you aren't improving and moving forward, you are falling behind because others are improving."

Yet many of today's crop of pros have intense drive to succeed, to improve. If some of them have bogeymen helping to drive them, there may be ample reasons. Here is a sampling:

- Nick Price's father died when he was 10.
- David Duval's brother died, despite an attempt to save him with a transplant of Dave's bone marrow; then his parents divorced.
- The fathers of Jack Nicklaus and Tiger Woods lived their dreams through their sons and drove them hard to succeed.
- Lee Trevino grew up fatherless and in poverty, living off golf bets.
- Se Ri Pak's coach/father was abusive and was an alleged small-town hoodlum.
- Ben Hogan's father died when he was nine.

- Arnold Palmer tried to impress his authoritarian father until the day his father died.
- Billy Casper had an absent father, then his parents divorced. He was constantly teased about his obesity.
- Bobby Jones was ill and nearly died as a child.
- Greg Norman and Sam Snead had distant fathers.
- Retief Goosen was nearly killed when struck by lightning as a teenager.

Many people believe all golf pros are from privileged families. However, it seems as though golfers at the very top often have an advantage over rivals with near or equal talent because they grew up with pressure, whether from the challenge of a dysfunctional home life or a missing or dominating parent. This can establish a mode by which they constantly want to prove themselves and to be resilient, even to seek out new challenges. And they learned to control their fear early, to recognize it and to realize, if only subconsciously, that pressure could help them. Perhaps, says University of Nebraska psychologist Richard Dienstbier, what doesn't kill you makes you stronger. "As they seek out and overcome more and more challenges, the tough should get tougher," he says. Many youths with a strong drive get into sports. "Sports is a breeding ground for youths looking to prove themselves," says sports psychologist Thomas Tutko, who has interviewed thousands of elite athletes. "It can give them attention and accolades and make them feel special, especially if they're from a large family," he said. "It can help children with psychological or emotional problems enhance their self-image."

Perhaps no one can say for certain if worry and emotional drive are largely responsible for the success of our top achievers.

Mental resiliency can vary from person to person, says sports psychologist James E. Loehr. Research suggests that some athletes may have a resilient genetic underpinning, which Loehr calls *mental toughness.*

After studying the lives of 500 such achievers throughout history, including scientists, politicians, business giants and athletes, including golfers Hogan and Nicklaus, I believe early environment has a strong influence. Of the 500, 72.4 percent came from a home with a serious parental problem, including 41 percent who had at least one parent die before they were 20. Some 31.6 percent had an absent, abusive or alcoholic parent and nearly nine percent were raised in poverty or watched their parents' finances collapse.

In many cases, the top male golfers seem to want to prove something to their fathers, such as Greg Norman has done, or at least they want to win for their dads, like Jack Nicklaus and Arnold Palmer. In his autobiography, *A Golfer's Life*, Palmer ended his story with a tribute to his late father, Deacon, who introduced him to golf as a tot at Latrobe County Club, which Arnie still owns, in the foothills of Pennsylvania's Allegheny Mountains. A statue of Deacon has been erected at the club and it constantly reminds Arnie how important his "Pap" was to his career and how he liked to make him proud. "Some things never change," Arnie says. "I still hope he'd be pleased."

If we have strong drives to please others, or simply to please ourselves, it is best if we attempt to examine and identify them. Once we are aware of something, we are in a position to try to alter or redirect our course of action.

"Golf is for smellin' heather and cut grass and walking fast across the countryside and feeling the wind and watching the sun go down and seein' your friends hit good shots and hittin' some yerself. It's love and feelin' the splendour o' this good world."

— *sports researcher and golf author Michael Murphy*

CHAPTER 12

DEVELOPING GOLF
SPIRITUALITY

A surefire way to reduce stress and choking on the golf course is to find pleasures besides scoring low. They abound if we look for them, but too often we do not. Instead, we are caught up in the games within our heads. When we stop and take time to look around, we appreciate our partners and all they have to offer, the beauty of nature and the ironic things going on all around us. But first we need to lose ourselves and our goals, to invest in things that are not so goal-oriented. This is a good way to reduce self-consciousness and ego and find some peace of mind while clutching that dreaded two-iron. Some people call this spirituality.

"What a beautiful place a golf course is," the late, legendary golf teacher Harvey Penick said. "From the meanest country pasture to the Pebble Beaches and St. Andrews of the world, a golf course is to me a holy ground. I feel God in the trees and grass and flowers, in the rabbits and the birds and the squirrels, in the sky and the water. I feel that I am home."

With this frame of mind, what does it matter if we shoot 68 or 108?

Not long ago, a women's club champion asked the advice of Terrence MacClure, an avid golfer, consultant and author of the book *Golf Ching*, which incorporates the philosophies of the ancient Chinese classic *I Ching*. The woman was playing so poorly, she had lost enjoyment in the game. MacClure suggested that the allure of trying to play well, trying to win the championship, had become so great, it had swept the woman aside and she could not focus on anything else. He advised that she focus more on the people she would play with, to encourage them with her game and the confidence they believed she had. Lo and behold, a month later she reported that enjoyment had returned to her game because she suddenly realized that others loved playing with her. The woman began playing in an effortless way, which MacClure attributed to "a deeper understanding of her game."

If, like that woman, you are feeling too much pressure to score or to perform, MacClure offers this advice: "You may be expecting too much from only one part of your game. Try to have a more balanced game by paying attention to other aspects of it." This balance includes bringing others into the mix. "Your game is important to other players. You're part of the golf community," MacClure added. "Golf communities exist for intimacy, love, bonding, assistance, survival, growth and mutual support. The golf community is there to follow your life. Your association with your group has advantages for all players in the golf community. This is a time to demonstrate your higher feelings toward your golf community: natural affections, openness and generosity."

"Golf is a game as much about the camaraderie, the walk together, as it is about flailing away at that little dimpled ball," says Andrew Shanley, a former caddy and author of the book *Fathers, Sons and Golf*. "On the course, we are respectful of the struggle others make to stay calm in the face of adversity. We know how hard it is to be focused when the mind is inclined to recall a million helpful tips, or to intrude with recollections of problems at home or office. That's why golf encourages courtesy and thoughtfulness, and why golfers are so careful on the greens not to walk across another player's line ... in extending goodwill to our fellow players, and in receiving their own in return, our travails are made bearable and our triumphs increase in pleasure. This becomes sort of a lesson in love; we see that by extending ourselves, we are rewarded with something very positive."

Complimenting your partners spreads the goodwill around, according to sports psychologist Terry Orlick. "We feel lots of good things about other people that we never share with them. These are often things that could give a lift to their day (as well as our own)."

Practising Embarrassment

If self-consciousness and embarrassment are two of your problems at the golf course — and they are for many duffers — there are two ways to reduce these feelings so they do not affect your game so harshly. The most popular way, of course, is to avoid being embarrassed by becoming a more proficient golfer, to practise hard and reduce the risk of poor shotmaking.

The second way is to *practise embarrassment*. By deliberately putting yourself in embarrassing situations, you will make the often-stark feelings of your emergency fear system more manageable. And you may become more humble and less defensive. When you examine the issue, it is not really our emergency fear system that is the enemy in golf; rather, it is the things we allow ourselves to respond to, the situations we allow this system to attack — threats to our ego, pride and self-esteem. As we have seen, most often our emergency fear system turns against us in the form of tension and excessive nervousness. And then we see it as the enemy, which is quite ironic, because nature intended it to be our ally. If we want to reduce this self-destruction, deliberately putting ourselves into vulnerable situations can show us that becoming embarrassed is not so bad after all. We can get used to the feelings and come to realize that our pride and ego can survive.

This, of course, can be about as easy as holing a bunker shot. Throughout our lives, we are encouraged to avoid situations that make us emotionally uncomfortable, beginning with our parents, who tried to protect us from feeling bad, who may have picked us up too much as babies every time we cried. Jerome Kagan, a developmental psychologist at Harvard University, conducted a study that revealed that overly sensitive and fearful children tended to become shy adults. Little wonder that, as a society in general, we deal poorly with situations involving pressure and fear. But Kagan concluded that such children can manage and even overcome their fears by being allowed to face them, by not being coddled too much by the parents.

Perhaps we would not feel so self-conscious if we got some practice deliberately shooting badly, then watching people's reactions ... but more importantly *our own* reaction. Fear feels uncomfortable largely because we have not learned how to deal with it. We don't like embarrassing situations or confrontations with ourselves or others because of the feelings they evoke. But unless we get used to them, we won't consistently perform well under pressure. That's why many players look unbeatable on the driving range, then falter in the heat of battle, says Dean Atkinson, golf director at Predator Ridge Golf Resort in Vernon, British Columbia; he conducts small wagers with his amateur and professional clients to keep them aroused during practice.

As an occasional player and medium-to-high handicapper, I worry about flubbing a shot. In the mid-1990s at a public course in Brampton, Ontario, I knocked three straight tee shots a total of 30 yards (that's 10 yards apiece). I'm sure I turned red in the face in front of my partners, my teenaged son Kevin and two strangers, at least on the first topped ball. The second and third ones were annoying, as well, but what helped me get over it was the fact that all three balls landed in a bushy area to the left of the tee (you could hardly call a 10-yard shot a hook). I might have left one errant ball to be found by another hacker, but not three. If I had left three behind, that would prove to my partners just how humiliated I was. Anyway, in my walk to find them, I glanced over at my three partners, who seemed slightly embarrassed. But they were not mocking me. They were embarrassed *for me*. Once I saw that, I didn't feel nearly so bad. In fact, I couldn't help but laugh. Then they laughed and we got on with our round. For the next 17 holes, I had a chance to prove I was not as bad a golfer as I had been on the first hole — and I did. The lesson was that I survived that potentially enormous embarrassment. From then on, I figured I could survive anything the game could throw at me.

But why should we wait for these rosy-faced moments? We can prepare our reaction by deliberately shooting poorly. Try it first on the practice range — top some tee shots and look around for people's responses. If anyone does react, it will likely be to acknowledge that they, too, have been in that situation. Talk to them about it. Laugh at yourself.

You can even evoke embarrassment and arousal through thoughts. Pretend you are Greg Norman, suffering down the back nine in blowing a big lead in the 1996 Masters. Imagine the pressure he felt and, if you visualize and relate strongly enough, you might feel a queasiness in your stomach or tension in your arms or shoulders. This is the same type of feeling you might get watching a sad or scary movie; if you relate enough to the character, you feel for him. If this sounds contrary to positive thinking, it is, in a way. And yet, as psychologist Martin Seligman says, it is important to learn to deal with the negative. If we continually avoid so-called negative feelings and reactions, we will never be able to manage them effectively. If you do want to read a book chocked full of positive thinking, hundreds of good ones are available, beginning with *The Power of Positive Thinking* by Norman Vincent Peale.

Facing Your Fears

Facing your fears on the golf course accomplishes several things. It eventually desensitizes you to what you are afraid of, it gets you accustomed to the physiological feelings of arousal, and it may raise your threshold for playing golf under arousal.

Tiger Woods says he performs better in the majors because he simulated pressure as a child. "When I was a little kid, I'd pretend I was Jack Nicklaus or Tom Watson on the back nine and in contention. I'd practise under pressure all the time when nobody was watching, and I still do." Of course, his father, Earl, exposed young Tiger to pressure and distractions. "I put him through Woods Finishing School," Earl said. "I would jingle the change in my pocket before he attempted to putt, or pump the brake on the golf cart before his backswing on an iron shot. It was psychological warfare — I wanted to make sure he would never run into anybody who was tougher mentally than he was, and we achieved that. He developed nerves of steel." (After he turned pro, Tiger did become agitated with the clicking of photographers' cameras, but that seemed more an issue of golf etiquette.)

Experience under pressure helped Matt Gogel win the 2002 AT&T Pebble Beach Pro-Am after he had blown a seven-shot lead in the final round of the same event two years earlier. "I learned a lot from that, how to collect myself under the gun," he said.

We learn that we become different people under pressure, because our emergency fear system activates with its powerful hormones and added strength and concentration. Dan Forsman discovered this while contending in the 1993 Masters and playing in a group with Nicklaus. The putter was suddenly feeling different in Forsman's hands because he was shaking with nervousness. Nicklaus recognized his partner's dilemma and winked at him. "It's something, isn't it?" Nicklaus said of Forsman's fear reaction. Forsman later recalled, "Here was the greatest golfer ever, and even he has those moments where the club does not feel the same because of the pressure." Of course, Nicklaus learned to deal with the pressure en route to winning six Masters!

"As we are exposed repeatedly to something that, for whatever reason, is frightening to us, we become progressively less and less afraid," says psychiatrist and golf consultant Phil Lee, who calls this practice *behavioural therapy*. Fear releases what Lee calls "anxiety chemicals" — hormones such as adrenaline, dopamine and noradrenaline — into our system, making it difficult to execute a golf shot. "The chemicals cause you to do badly, and then you release more chemicals in the future. Bad results lead to justifiably increased fear about future results. And more fear means more chemicals."

Behavioural therapy offers a way to turn this reflex off, Lee says. "Everyone has panic attacks ... but everyone knows that if you keep getting up on a horse after being thrown, it gets a little less scary." Lee says that everyone has a body faucet that remains shut until they feel fear, then the anxiety chemicals spew throughout your bloodstream as part of the emergency fear system. The more you expose yourself to fearful situations, the less fear you will feel, and gradually the anxiety chemicals will decrease.

However, at the highest levels of competition, some golfers like to use this *fear energy* for enhanced power and concentration, so they choose to try and raise their optimal levels of arousal during practice and tournaments. John Anderson, a sports psychologist who works with Olympic athletes, says that Woods and superstars in other sports, such as Michael Jordan in basketball and the Williams sisters in tennis, can sometimes perform effectively on an arousal scale of 10 out of 10. "But you have to be careful you don't get beyond an arousal curve that is comfortable to you," he said. "As you continue to experience pressure, you begin to understand more and more where your point is. You may discover you can learn to handle six out of 10, but if you go beyond that and you haven't been there before, you begin to worry. Then you forget to trust your internal system and focus on external things. Then the arousal state is not functional." Anderson added that raising this threshold seems better suited for athletes in football, track and field, and hockey and not so much for golf.

On lower competitive levels, if golfers want to get used to the feelings of arousal, they should seek games with better partners, or play in high-stakes tournaments. "You learn to deal with pressure against great golfers week after week, and you learn how to win," says Dave Hemstad of Thornhill, Ontario, who attended Southwest Missouri State on a golf scholarship.

Serious golfers also expose themselves to fearful shot situations, which can lead to choking. Gary Player has spent a good portion of his life whacking balls out of sand traps in practice while pretending he was saving par in the British Open. Lee Trevino and Laura Davies raise their pressure levels through betting on shots. As a child, Becky Iverson chipped shots over her house (can you imagine the pressure of Mom finding a broken window?). Frank Dobbs of St. Lucie, Florida, an assistant pro at the Club Med Sandpiper, puts extra pressure on himself in a casual round. "All my life, every time I went out, I was playing a match against my brother or playing my dad. And so I've learned to accept whatever happens to me out there on the golf course."

If distractions and noises create pressure for you, you might want to simulate it by training next to a loud radio. If you have a pressure job, you may be able to transfer some of your skills to the golf course. Judith Allan-Kyrinis, always a contender in Ontario amateur golf, says that her job as a nurse at Toronto General Hospital helps her deal with pressures on the greens.

Golf and God

For many golf pros, spirituality has a more tangible meaning. Prayer has become a key strategy for an increasing number of PGA players who say their faith helps them deal with the pressures of an emotionally draining game that has been sometimes described as hell.

An estimated 54 of the top 125 PGA players have attended at least one session of a travelling weekly Bible study. Some of the tour's top names have been speakers at the National Golf Ministry, a branch of the Fellowship of Christian Athletes, including U.S. Open winner Steve Jones, two-time majors winner Mark O'Meara, Davis Love III, Loren Roberts, Tom Lehman and Trevor Dodds.

Public talk of God is not as prevalent in golf as it is in the National Football League, where players often motion to the heavens after scoring a touchdown. But a subculture of PGA Christians became known in 1999 when born-again Christian Payne Stewart died in a plane crash.

Since Stewart's funeral, many PGA players have worn bracelets inscribed with "What Would Jesus Do?" which Stewart was wearing at the time of his death.

Mostly, though, pro golfers do not preach to others, according to 1987 Masters winner and practising Christian Larry Mize. "We are not pushy," he said. "We don't try to force anybody to come to our weekly Bible studies ... but the tour can be a lonely place. It helps when I have fellow believers out there for me." Rather, Mize said, theirs is a personal decision, which gets them through pressure situations. "I still get nervous in golf, but it is a totally different pressure I feel. My satisfaction and security and significance are in Christ rather than in the results of my game. He has given me more patience and dedication. And yet, I have more reason to win now, and glorify God."

Tour veteran Scott Simpson claims his faith helped him win the 1987 U.S. Open. "The week before, I was frustrated with my game, but the day before the tournament, our Bible study focused on how true contentment comes from Jesus Christ. Instead of worrying, I thanked God that I was fortunate just to be playing in the tournament. And it took pressure off. My faith helps me because I don't need to worry about being embarrassed."

Loren Roberts, who grew up Presbyterian, says a prayer sparked him to win his first tournament, the 1994 Bay Hill Invitational. He recalls his prayer while standing over an important 40-foot putt: "Lord, just let me hit this putt to the best of my ability. I am not going to pray that You make it for me; I know I've got to hit it. Just give me the strength to make my best effort and accept the consequences." Roberts drained the putt for the victory.

And yet Roberts got a different result at the 1994 U.S. Open. Needing just a four-foot putt to win the championship, he said the same prayer, then hit "the worst putt of my life, and it didn't even come close." He looked upon that miss as a learning experience, that it was up to him, not God, to make the shots.

Three-time tour winner Gary Hallberg said prayer got him into the zone when he needed to finish second in a tournament to retain his PGA card. "From the first tee, I let go," he said. "I wasn't controlling it. It's hard to explain, but I went out there and floated along. I finished second and got my card. He [God] did it. And I've played better since that day."

Religion brings some golfers back to a peaceful state of mind, like PGA player Pat Bates, who writes a different Bible verse number on his ball each week (part of the reason, though, is that he once accidentally hit someone else's golf ball by mistake).

Not everyone agrees with religion on tour. A tour veteran, who asked to remain anonymous, said golfers should take total responsibility for their play and learn to deal with pressure shots with their own fortitude. "I am not against anyone having his own beliefs, for certain, but this is a game where you live and die as an individual," he said. "It toughens you. [Religion] can be a type of crutch."

The LPGA Tour has an informal gathering of Christians who meet for weekly prayer, often led by hall-of-famer Betsy King.

Barbara Bunkowsky Scherbak, who was brought up Lutheran, had a "born again" experience in 1986 when she was struggling with alcohol and other problems on tour. "I was on the path to destruction," she said. "So I went to be with a group of Christians on tour." Scherbak said her faith has made her golf more disciplined. "I used to quit when I'd start playing badly. Now, with the Lord, I'm at peace. When things start going badly, I can make light of it. I don't take life so seriously. I'm not so hard on myself."

"They tell me this game is supposed to be fun.

When?"

— *Thom Geishauser of Altoona, Pennsylvania*

CHAPTER 13

ENJOYING THINGS OTHER THAN THE SCORE

When tension, pressure or boredom appear, it may take a dose of fun to make golf worthwhile again. Fun may even ease choking and keep at bay the dreaded yips. There is a time to take the game seriously, especially for professionals and other elite players, but too much intensity can ruin a five-hour round.

"It's easy for recreational golfers to forget that golf is just a game played primarily for the purpose of escaping, unwinding and having fun," says psychologist Alan Shapiro. "To forget that, even though golf has the power to elicit the full gamut of emotions and even though you can learn about yourself and grow as a person from your experience as a golfer, it still remains a game."

Golf psychologist Patrick J. Cohn says that if golf isn't enjoyable anymore, if years of playing and practice make you lethargic, you should remember the reasons why you enjoyed the game in the first place. "Do you like the physical activity?" he said. "Do you enjoy golf because you enjoy striking a ball properly and the feeling that brings? Do you play to socialize and be with other people? Do you enjoy being in the outdoors? The next time you feel frustrated, angry, tired or stale, remember why you enjoy playing." Cohn recommends that golfers enjoy the moment. "You must stop and smell the roses. Most golf courses are on the most beautiful pieces of land. Research on flow and motivation reveals that people gain enjoyment from just participating in the activity for itself. It does not have to be dependent on rewards, recognition or praise from others."

Ian Baker-Finch reached the height of competitive golf, winning the 1991 British Open, but partly through nervousness, he missed 32 consecutive cuts at tournaments. "I was hooking the ball from fear," he said. Now, between television broadcasts, commentator Baker-Finch plays up to 36 holes a day for sheer enjoyment. "I just love golf so much."

Of course, competitive golf is often more fun if you are scoring well, like Sergio Garcia was doing in the 1999 PGA Championship when he ran up a fairway and danced in the air as he challenged Tiger Woods. But Garcia always looks like he's having a ball (apart from a brief period in 2002 when he waggled his backswing up to 30 times because of nerves). Maybe because in 1999 he was still a teenager. Maybe we can learn from him.

Enjoy the Process

Too much competition seems to take the pleasure out of golf for some people. "If you feel that the joy and satisfaction of competition can happen only when the game is over — the praise and status that you get if you win — I believe that you will always feel a tremendous amount of pressure and have a hard time playing up to your ability," says golf teacher Fred Shoemaker. "A

PRESSURE RELIEVER: PLAY GAMES

The following are a few games you can use as alternates from your usual medal play. They are taken from the book *Golf Games Within the Game* by Linda Valentine and Margie Hubbard.

- **Bunkers** — Before teeing off on each hole, players must select one bunker to play through before reaching the green. Think of the sand practice!
- **Chapman** — Two partners each play a ball, alternately hitting one another's shots; on the green, only their best of two balls is played.
- **Chip-in** — Each golfer pays 25 cents or more to enter; as soon as somebody chips in from off the green, he or she collects the pot, which carries over from hole to hole.
- **Distraction** — Use a noise or distraction (but not physical) during the swing of a partner; one per hole.
- **Eighteen** — On the practice putting green, try to score 18 points first. Score three points for a one-putt and two points for closest to the hole; if you exceed 18, you are penalized the amount for which you have gone over.
- **Hangtime** — Using a stopwatch, time the longest time in the air off the tee; these times can be accumulated throughout the round to come up with a winner.
- **Hate 'em** — Before teeing off, circle two holes that you absolutely hate, and subtract the score on these two holes from your total; or you can toss out your worst three holes (any holes decided after the round).
- **Humility** — When you lose a hole, you have to carry a partner's bag until you win another hole.
- **Pick your pro partner** — Pick a pro partner from the list of that week's PGA or LPGA tournament, just those who made the cut after 36 holes; then add the score of his or her next round to your score that day and compare it to that of your partner and his or her fantasy player.

golfer's experience consists of a triangle of performance, learning and enjoyment. If these elements are in balance, they all work well. But if they are out of balance, each one suffers. The secret to competing successfully is being aware that the games of learning and enjoyment are under your control and winning them will give you the best chance of winning the scoring game, since it will ensure your best performance."

Having fun can sometimes allow you to relax and to score better. "To play your best golf, you need to be having fun," said PGA veteran Scott Simpson. "When I am enjoying myself and letting it happen, I play to my ability."

Even at the highest competitive level, golf is a game of play, not work, says golf psychologist Robert K. Winters. "Many golfers find themselves frustrated ... after putting in long hours on the practice range, the game they love starts to feel like hard, manual labour. They need to create fun in practice sessions and find ways to have fun on the course. It is important to remember not to take yourself too seriously."

After a pair of 76s in the 1988 U.S. Open, Peter Jacobsen said he felt like "an old lawn mower that wouldn't turn over. I just couldn't get started ... I decided to just go out and have some fun." In the third round, a loose Jacobsen went out and fired a 64.

The great Bobby Jones retired from major competitive golf at age 28 in 1930 because he got tired of constantly competing. It was said that he once got so stressed, he lost 18 pounds in a tournament. "It [a championship] is something like a cage," he said. "First you are expected to get into it and then you are expected to stay there. But, of course, nobody can stay there. Out you go — and then you are trying your hardest to get back in again. Rather silly, isn't it, when golf — just golf — is so much fun?"

PGA player Mike Reid believes adult golfers lose their sense of fun when they become too analytical. "Adults are too analytical. Go back and remember what you loved about the game when you were a kid," he said. "Don't forget, this is supposed to be fun."

In his prime, Arnold Palmer was the ultimate competitor and yet he enjoyed the beauty of the game as well as his mastery of it. Arnie said, "What other people may find in poetry or art museums, I find in the flight of a good drive — the white ball sailing up into the blue sky, growing smaller and smaller, then suddenly reaching its apex, curving, falling and finally dropping to the turf to roll some more, just the way I planned it."

If you are an occasional player, why not be satisfied with several very good shots in each round?

ADDICTIVE FUN

If you play more than three rounds of golf a week, you may be addicted to the game. When you spend so much time at any hobby, it's possible you are addicted to the pleasure (or rush) it gives you, either psychologically or chemically, says stress researcher Dr. Archibald Hart. The chemical component can be the hormone endorphin, which makes us feel good after a good shot. Such addictions can become harmful if they interfere with the other things going on in our lives (such as our golf widows or widowers). Rock star Alice Cooper is a confessed golf junkie, playing more than 300 rounds a year.

Golf as Life

I have learned much about getting more out of golf from watching my father-in-law, Tony Vanderklei. You won't find Tony getting frustrated very often, even though he has played in an

PRESSURE RELIEVER: SEEK GOLF'S OTHER PLEASURES

If we are too concerned with the potential result of our shot, we sometimes don't stop to drink in golf's other pleasures. Some things we should take time to cherish besides the score:

- The flag flapping in the breeze, 160 yards away.
- The swoosh of the ball as it leaves your clubface.
- Closing your eyes to smell the freshly mown fairway, listening to the crickets, the larks or the babbling stream, rejoicing in the fact they don't care about your mistakes.
- Walking onto the dance floor with your putter in hand.
- Replacing your divot; watch how it fits into the hole you left like the last piece of nature's jigsaw puzzle.
- The sound of the ball plopping into the bottom of the cup; or is that the sound of relief?
- Noticing that players of all genders, ages and cultures are on the course.
- The soft rain, how it adds another level of experience and challenge.
- Standing at the tee box, waiting for the group ahead to get out of range, knocking dirt from your spikes, squinting into the sun, picking your club out of the bag, getting ready for the challenge.
- The ball launched into the air against the blue sky — your ball.
- The reactions of your partners to their games, especially the ironic twists golf can offer.
- The anticipation of the stories, as well as the cold drink going down the back of your throat, waiting for you in the clubhouse.

industrial golf league for 27 years. He balances his weekly competition — and keeps the game in perspective — by also playing noncompetitive golf pretty much every day, spring through fall, with Al Narus and Mike Barbara at the Rio Vista Golf Club in Fort Erie, Ontario.

Rio Vista is no Pebble Beach. It has winter rules year-round, with 3,200 yards over nine holes. But it is hard to imagine a better game than the one this threesome plays, with little tension or choking. For a senior membership of $460, they get their money's worth. "Usually we tee off at 7:30 every morning," Tony explains. "We enjoy it because this course has a lot of guys like us. We have about the same handicap [nine] and our outlook on life and our language are the same; happy-go-lucky with a lot of needling. We even talk sometimes when the other guy is in the middle of his backswing."

The daily fun is also a great social outlet for the three retirees.

Tony Vanderklei is 80 at this writing, a former tool engineer and manager in the aircraft industry. Eighty-three-year-old Barbara worked for a Buffalo, N.Y., paint company and 92-year-old Narus was a pastry cook in the U.S. Navy. "We don't act our ages, and I think the game is partly responsible for that," Tony says. "When retirement comes, you not only lose your daily activities but your contact with society. Golf is a great substitute, a way to fraternize."

When he took up golf at age 38, Tony was more serious and, because he was a department manager, "There was a type of status quo. I felt I had to live up to my status and not expose any weaknesses in my game." But that intensity has eased and now Rio Vista gets a lot of mentions in Tony's daily diary: the day he won a closest-to-the-hole coffee and had a canteen suddenly drive up to the green; his tee shot on October 2, 1992, which hit the flag and dropped into the cup, costing him four pitchers of beer in the clubhouse; and the Sunday morning that Brownie Porter stopped breathing and died on the No. 9 tee.

"Golf is like life; everything happens out there on the course," Tony says. "So you may as well enjoy it while it lasts."

SIGNS OF TROUBLE

The top 10 signs that you have become too serious about golf:

10. You have trouble getting your glove off because your fingers are shaking.
9. You are constantly updating your score before you have finished a hole.
8. Your scorecards are taking over your desk at home.
7. You know everyone else's handicap.
6. Your putter has more shine than your car.
5. You go out of your way to learn that damn greenskeeper's name.
4. You remember the anniversary you broke 90 with greater ease than you remember your wedding anniversary.
3. You have to change the grips on your clubs often, from holding them too tight.
2. You stop yelling "fore!", hoping to bean somebody in the adjoining fairway so it will keep your shot from going out of bounds.
1. Your partners stop yelling "Fore!" when a ball is headed for you.

STRATEGY NO. 3:
FOCUS

We've discussed in Section II some things to make the pressure of your overall golf game more manageable; now it's time to get down to some specifics. This section explores the concept of focus, particularly the ability to ignore pressure and fear by means of concentrating on the shot at hand. Chapter 14 discusses one of the cardinal rules of successful golf: learning to trust yourself and your swing. In Chapter 15, we examine in detail the subject of focus, including strategies from the great golf minds. The ultimate type of focus — a magical state known as "flow" — is the subject of Chapter 16. Chapter 17 looks at what golfers might do between shots to lessen the pressure on their upcoming shot. Chapter 18 discusses focus for the special shots on the first tee and the short game.

"If you're analyzing every shot for mechanical flaws, sooner or later you're going to find some and it's going to be very difficult for you to trust."

— Tom Kite

CHAPTER 14

TRUSTING YOURSELF AND YOUR SWING

Pro golfers John Daly and Laura Davies are bigger than life and bring attention to themselves with their long drives and their emotional reactions. In the off-season, they could probably go bear hunting with a stick. Who could imagine that this dynamic duo would become afraid of hitting a golf ball? But at times during the 2000 and 2001 seasons, they did. They stopped trusting themselves and their swings, which became tentative and wayward.

"I became so frightened of taking a full swing, I would nearly freeze at the top of my backswing," Davies admitted. Her game suffered so much, she sought advice from the only person she thought understood her plight — the colourful Daly, who had learned to start trusting himself again and simplified his game after a terrible slump. (For a variety of reasons, the two-time majors winner had gone five years without a victory, but in 2001, he improved from number 507 to 47 in the world rankings.) Daly told Davies to go back to doing what they both did best: "grip it and rip it." Davies did, and suddenly she started playing with more confidence and skill, snapping a streak of 23 successive tournaments without a victory.

Unheralded Rich Beem used this philosophy to produce a stunning upset in the 2002 PGA Championship at Hazeltine National Golf Club in Minneapolis, trusting himself enough to remain aggressive in the final round to stare down Tiger Woods' challenge. Beem used his driver more than any player in the field on Hazeltine's narrow fairways.

When we talk about focus in golf, the first thing we need to do is trust ourselves and our golf swing. If you allow yourself trust, you can slip more easily into the cocoon of focus. If you do not, your self-doubt and subsequent tension will become huge distractions to your concentration.

"Trusting is the hardest thing," says PGA player Stuart Appleby. One of our biggest fears, and one of the most common reasons for choking, is the thing we do 70 to 100 times in a round — swing the club. Trusting *yourself* may be even harder at times.

The best teaching pros hammer away with such phrases as, "Just train it and trust it." Just stop fretting about everything you've learned at the driving range and, when you get to the course, let it fly. Piece of cake, eh? Many amateur golfers tell me their game seems just dandy at the range, but deteriorates on the course when score is counted and other people are watching. Then their trust becomes a little shaken. And they become trussed. Even pros report this drop in confidence at times. "The high handicappers who I see in clinics tend to be people tying themselves in knots, physically and mentally," says Bob Rotella. "But pro or amateur, whatever their specific concerns are, they all know one thing. They're better players than they're showing on the golf course and in tournaments."

You must learn to trust what you have learned if you are to improve on the golf course or in tournaments; otherwise, fear of your own swing can become the biggest fear, the biggest distraction and certainly the biggest cause of choking. But with work and patience, it can be mastered. Don't believe the naysayers, including that doubting one who lives in the caddy shack in the back of your head.

Look at other areas of your life in which you have gained enough confidence that you simply go on faith. You hop onto a bicycle and balance down the street without thinking that your safety hinges on narrow strips of rubber. You get behind the wheel of a 2,000-pound car and drive 100 km/h in traffic without thinking too much of the mechanics of your steering and your footwork on the floor.

So what is the big deal about standing above a golf ball and letting the club fly without analyzing your swing or without being self-conscious?

Muscle Memory

First of all, you must develop some trust (and its close relative, *confidence*) on the practice range, away from the scoring, the expectations and the prying eyes. Most swing doctors agree that technique must be fashioned and problems fixed on the range, and on the links. "Ultimately all the hard work you put into your game will pay off — your natural instincts will take over and you'll be in what the tour players call the zone," says David Leadbetter, instructor to golf's superstars.

In any difficult activity, you must practise hard, then trust your motor skills to carry it out in pressure situations without having your emergency fear system kick in. That complex and powerful system is always ready, always looking for a natural response in what is an unnatural game. But we can at least make its responses second nature through our thinking and our training, our muscle memory. Pianists do it every day; think of them making just one finger misstep while playing Beethoven in front of an audience. Typists know there is a lot of pressure when working to deadline. I can type about 125 words a minute — sometimes more when I'm under the gun — and yet decades ago I forgot where the individual keys were. My subconscious mind knows, however. And that is one of the keys of trust: let your subconscious mind, in which you have programmed skills, take over. The old autopilot.

Sure, it's a leap of faith when you consider the golf swing has so little room for error. Trusting your swing under pressure is even more difficult. "It takes courage and mental toughness to count on yourself to make your normal swing when the pressure's on, " said Sam Snead, who was sure enough of himself enough to win 81 PGA tournaments. "But I know it's the best way not to allow the demons to take over and jump at the ball."

But golfers with technically poor swings do learn to trust their swings, warts and all, and sometimes get good results. Jovey M. Eala, a doctor from the Philippines, wrote to me after one of my psychology columns appeared on the internet. "I am a high handicapper. Over here, a lot of golfers have unorthodox styles of swing, but we still get some good scores." On the Champions Tour, Allen Doyle flourishes despite an awkward swing — flat from practising as a youth in a room with low ceilings.

As far as carrying that trust from the range to the golf course, remember the discussions earlier in this book about not focusing so much on score, and certainly not about what other people think. If you worry too much about those things, if your pride is wrapped up in a golf swing, you may need to examine your motives and goals.

But let's examine how to trust your swing. It's hard to have total faith in a technique when so many things can go haywire (you don't have to backtrack to Chapter 4 to know that), not to mention what the weather and course conditions may do to your little ball. Yet your shot will go askew more often if you don't trust the swing. Any hesitation or self-doubt will be felt and repeated by your golf ball as it sails off course.

When they don't trust their swing, some golfers try to over-control their shots. "What typically happens when you lose trust is that you hold on and don't release the club," says Patrick Cohn. "Others don't transfer their weight and stay back on their rear foot, and still others stab at the ball and stick their club in the ground." Golfers must identify these problems before they can do anything about them, he added.

PRESSURE RELIEVER: YOUR TRUSTY CLUB

Some golfers have faith in one club more than others and they trust them whenever they are in trouble. In fact, today's golf clubs can be trusted much more than those in the past. Manufacturers have spent millions of dollars creating state-of-the-art clubs that will get the ball up into the air — if you let them.

A final point: going out to the course with the idea of having fun will probably help you trust your swing. When people become immersed in something they have fun doing, they tend not to think so much, or suffer as many doubts. This is sometimes called the *flow* state (see Chapter 16).

Swing Thoughts

Many instructors believe golfers swing best when they have just one or two thoughts before swinging, or when they don't think at all. "The fact is," says sports psychologist Bob Rotella, "most amateurs don't know exactly what breaks down when they swing badly. If they try to correct their swing, they usually wind up compounding the error. They would be far better off forgetting about their swing mechanics, thinking about appropriate targets and strategy, and making up their mind that they will shoot the best score possible with the swing they brought to the course that day."

David Leadbetter adds, "It is very easy to get caught up in the technical aspects of golf, and problems can arise when you try to combine working on your swing with working on your score. Out on the course, you must discipline yourself to let go of detailed theory. Flush your mind of unnecessary jargon; carry no more than two *swing keys* (thoughts) just to help reinforce your feel. Think of swinging the club rather than positioning." Good keys, Leadbetter added, would include "complete" or "swing to the finish" (if you are having problems following through). These keys will help your rhythm by keeping your body and mind relaxed, he added.

Butch Harmon teaches his students, including Tiger Woods, to "make a habit of always planting a positive image or thought into your mind just before you swing."

Another respected teacher, Jim Flick, wants his students to stop thinking altogether. "Hell, the last thing I want you doing when you're standing over the ball is thinking and giving yourself verbal commands," he said. "I'm leery of a single conscious thought that might introduce tension at precisely the moment when your body should be guided by routine and habit."

And, of course, if you want to get better you should play a lot. "When you don't play often, you're not comfortable trusting your swing," says broadcaster and Champions Tour winner Gary McCord.

Beginners have more trouble trusting themselves before they have developed a grooved swing that is comfortable, that works for them. "Attempting to learn a new skill is never natural at first," Patrick Cohn said. "All motor skills are learned at first by controlling movement and eventually skills become ingrained in memory. But a great deal of practice is necessary to reach this stage of automaticity. As you practise, you develop a stronger swing memory pattern in your mind (some people refer to this as *muscle memory*). This allows you to feel confident that you can hit the shot you call upon from memory."

Many amateurs in the three to eight handicap range suffer from *paralysis by over-analysis*, says PGA player Paul Azinger. "They probably read too many instruction articles and they'll never get any better. Sure, you need a key thought, but when they start hitting the ball badly, they get mechanical and start focusing on what they're doing wrong."

As you climb the competitive ladder, the pressure of winning a tournament may result in self-doubt, says Fred Funk, a five-time PGA winner. "But you've got to try not to think about the pressure," he said. "Trust that all the time you spent practising has brought you to this important shot."

When you trust your swing, you get out of your own way and prevent your emergency fear system from kicking in and becoming disruptive.

Our old nemesis, fear, can poison trust in your swing or your game, Cohn said. "Fear of being embarrassed, fear of losing a tournament and fear of the consequences of a poor shot can ruin a fluid and natural swing." That is where the emergency fear system kicks in to make our rhythm hiccup.

More than anyone, perfectionists have trouble trusting their swing. "High motivation is a positive quality in golf when it deals with being dedicated to working hard and practising," Cohn said. "But the main goal of a perfectionist is to make flawless swings, rather than getting the ball in the hole ... he develops habits without knowing what's happening."

Being cocky when they approach the ball helps many players believe in themselves. It encourages aggressive hormones such as noradrenaline and dopamine to be released into the system. Watch Karrie Webb stand over her shot in an almost condescending fashion. Larry Mize, 1987 Masters champion, believes that, when under pressure, taking a more aggressive swing than usual can help eliminate your nerves.

FOCUS TIP: WHOMP IT

The best example of a player trusting his swing, according to PGA veteran Peter Jacobsen, was Fred Couples in his prime. "He comes across at times as lackadaisical, carefree and non-analytical," Jacobsen said. "But what he is really tapping into is the essence of great golf, which is arriving at a zone of total relaxation and total confidence. He just steps up to the golf ball, takes a deep breath to relax, takes it back and whomps it. Then he goes and finds it and whomps it again. And when he adds up the whomps, the total is usually lower than the other 143 whompers."

When pressed about it, Couples said, "When I get ready for a shot, I just pull up my sleeves, shrug my shoulders and try to get relaxed. Then I remember the best shots I've hit in my life with whatever club I have in my hand at the time."

Faith and Your Swing

There is another way to look at trust: go on blind faith and simply let go. Whether it is trusting their technique or their ability, almost every elite golfer or elite athlete I've interviewed over the years has talked about *letting go* as being one of the key elements of good performance. There are other factors at work, for sure, but trust and confidence are vital to peak performance.

Psychiatrist Ned Hallowell compares a person's belief in the golf swing to a belief in God. "If you play golf or if you believe in God, you know that what is most important to both golf and religious belief is also what is most difficult: keeping your faith. I mean no disrespect in combining the sacred with the secular; instead I offer that there is a psychology common to both believers and non-believers. The lesson both God and golf teach is to let go. To keep faith, let go of control. Both the believer and the golfer have learned that a grander scheme will take over if they can let it. The best golf shots are hit unconsciously. You simply step up to the ball and let fly. Sure, you have taken lessons and practised in order to learn the basic swing."

Hallowell, a part-time golfer, says the people who worry the least usually have some sort of faith. He should know; he's written best-sellers about the subject, *Worry* and *Connect*. "They believe in God, or in nature, or in Buddha, or in the scientific method, or in their swing. They have learned how to let go of the need for total control ... Even if you hit bad shot after bad shot, you come back to your swing as your basic belief. You may tinker with your swing, practice it over and over, to get in shape for the big match. But when that day comes, you put aside your preparation and just swing. The more you let go, the better you do."

And the more you let go, the less you get in your own way.

Trust Your Ability to Shake off Failure

Let's say that on the No. 1 tee, you cannot trust yourself and the ball dribbles into the rough. So what? So what if you *fail* today? What is failure in your life, anyway? A poor score? A botched sand shot? If you've read this far, you understand the need to put the golf score into perspective. Failing is losing a whole year of school and not learning from it. Failing is giving up on a relationship without trying. Failing is an unwillingness to take opportunities in your life. Unless you are a touring professional, how can you equate a golf game with failing? When you trust your ability to survive a bad golf shot with other people watching, the pressure decreases significantly.

As golfers, we have more going for us than we think. If the only trust you needed was the swing itself, you might be in trouble because everybody's swing gets bugs in it from time to time. Several times during his sensational 2000 season, Tiger Woods got a glitch in his swing and yet he trusted his ability to bounce back, to grind through the problem, to win tournaments.

Trust in any type of motor skill begins with trust in yourself. If you trust yourself, you will bail yourself out time and time again. If you didn't have some trust in yourself, you wouldn't be at the golf course, standing around the first tee with all those fellow hackers watching you try to get the ball into the air. You've been in pressure situations before and have survived. You trusted yourself enough to come out to play this difficult game for four hours, to shell out $50 for green fees, not to mention hard-earned cash for equipment.

And then there is the trust in your ability to shake off failure, that if you happen to hit a bad shot, you will not get too embarrassed and you will survive to play another hole. Then there can be trust in your ability to grind out your golf game when your swing isn't clicking on all cylinders. Combinations of trusts, or even just one of them, can get you through a round even when you don't quite trust your swing.

Even when swing problems occur, players can grind through it and compensate with their short game. All the great swing masters have battled problems. "It's felt like I've been swinging an elephant's trunk," said Azinger about his swing problems on the 2000 PGA Tour. But such players battle their problems successfully because in the end they trust not only their swing, but their ability to find other ways to score. Golf is a game of grinding, where you can't trust that your shot will be perfect all the time, but you can trust your ability to bounce back from the rough or a hazard or a bad day.

The knowledge that they can be nervous and full of doubt and yet still prevail keeps players like Notah Begay III going. Coming down the stretch in the 1999 Michelob Championship at Kingsmill, Begay said he felt as if he was choking with emotion and anxiety. "I told my caddy I felt like I was suffocating. There's really no way to overcome it, except keep on driving through. It's like driving through smoke. You don't know what's on the other side. You just have to trust yourself and steer right through it."

"Choking is connected with losing the ability to

concentrate."

— Arnold Palmer

"To play any golf shot correctly requires an

unwavering concentration. The most perfect

swing in the world needs direction ... and when

the possessor begins to do a little daisy-picking,

something always goes wrong."

—Bobby Jones

CHAPTER 15

FOCUS:
Onesome Golf

F ocus is crucial to the success, not to mention the enjoyment, of any activity. In golf, focus separates excellence
from mediocrity. Confidence and relaxation are cardinal,
too, but often they do not fall into place until focus is achieved.
Determination, inspiration and a beautiful swing are all negated
if you don't focus them properly. We can look at focus from
Bobby Jones' "negative" angle or we can see it in a different light:
Effective focus can make up for a lot of deficiencies in your game.

Any discussion about choking or peak performance eventually
leads to focus. If you pay close attention to what you are doing,
you will flourish and you will not become self-conscious (which
can unleash your emergency fear system). When you focus
properly, everything wonderful has a chance of falling into place
and distractions fade, sand traps, noises, your scorecard and your
worries. Single-mindedness wins. "He's like a onesome out
there," said Tommy Armour III of Tiger Woods and his steely
concentration.

The problem is, human beings are not singular. We are complex, with numerous issues and problems. The narrower we can focus down these issues, the more chance we have of smiling when we check our scorecard at the end of the round. Focus is about disciplining yourself to keep attention on what is important, but it may not come to you naturally. "Focus is not an easy skill to acquire, especially for the average golfer, who may not even be aware of why they should try to focus their concentration," says golf psychologist Gary Golbesky of Ann Arbor, Michigan. "I believe this is a learned skill, to focus one's attention on what is most relevant at the time. Learning not to be bothered by distractions is another skill to learn, which is more of a cognitive approach of assessing why something bothers us."

The most effective type of concentration is one of relaxation, in which we become so absorbed in our shot that tension is not an issue. But that is another paradox of this crazy game — to be easy and eager at the same moment. Not tense, but *intense*. "You need to take your time with shots, but also be intense about them and not take them lightly," says LPGA player Mardi Lunn.

THREE FOCUS TIPS

In his book *The Inner Game of Golf*, W. Timothy Gallwey highlights three steps in reaching effective concentration:

- **Discipline**: Make a disciplined effort to focus your attention.
- **Interest**: Concentration reaches a deeper level when the mind becomes interested in its focus.
- **Absorption**: Reach a deepening level of interest to the point you begin to lose yourself in your shot.

Marlin M. MacKenzie, a counsellor to amateur and professional athletes, teaches golfers to see the golf ball so clearly as to make it very white and bright, making it a better target. When golfers see it fuzzy, their shots tend to go off course, he said. (And yet, researchers have found that focusing *too hard* can cause choking, as well.)

Focus Cues

Don't panic if you can't master focus completely. Tom Watson says even the pros lose their concentration for four or five shots every round. "Over a four-day tournament, even if every lapse costs you just one stroke, that's 16 to 20 shots a week, and that's the difference between being the leading money winner and losing your card," Watson said. When your focus slips, there are ways to snap back to attention. A cue can be effective — a word you say to yourself ("reload!") or something you force yourself to look at (a sticker on your bag) or a tune you whistle to yourself. When she felt herself falling out of the lead in the 2000 Ontario Amateur Women's Golf Championship, Laura Henderson snapped her fingers to get herself out of a bogey slide. It worked and she went on to win the title; then, in 2001, she helped the University of Georgia win the NCAA Women's Division I championship.

In my own amateur golf game, when I go through periods of not being able to focus on impact with the ball, I let out a grunt, just like tennis players do when hitting the ball. Many pros talk to themselves when they have lost concentration. At the 2000 U.S. Women's Open, Karrie Webb found her mind wandering ahead several holes as she racked up birdies and increased her lead. Later she recalled, "I get ahead of myself sometimes. It happened a few times today. I just have to talk to myself every now and then. I have to calm myself and think about the shot at hand, not the next hole or five holes ahead."

Staying in the present is a priority of focusing properly. In fact, one of my definitions of pressure is when the past (thoughts of previous bad shots) and the future (worries about a potential miss) come together to disrupt the present.

PGA veteran Richard Zokol found a technique for staying in the present that he calls the "units of execution." Zokol rates every shot he takes — from unsatisfactory to excellent — and once a shot has been taken, he detaches himself from it and goes on to rate the next shot, giving it equal importance. In other words, he doesn't think about an eight-foot putt being for birdie or for par (we all know how much tougher that length of a par putt can be). But with his own scoring system, Zokol approaches the birdie and par putts the same way.

A Controlled Environment: The Pre-shot Routine

The key to focus, says University of Minnesota golf coach John Means, is "routine, routine, routine. Once you have a pre-shot routine down, you overcome choking." It is a mini-environment, a place to step in and out of, where we focus only on the shot. We need to keep each shot a separate entity and the pre-shot routine celebrates that for about 20 minutes out of a four-hour round. Because we can focus intently only for so long, it is best that we move in and out of our mindset, relaxing when we are out of it and becoming more intense when we are inside its bubble.

We will never focus out all the pressure and arousal of a competitive round; much of that we will bring to our game subconsciously. If anything, we can try to redirect that energy as part of our focus, to get the arousal hormones working for us rather than against us, as with anxiety. The subconscious fits nicely into the pre-shot routine; it turns off your conscious mind and allows your routine, muscle memory and training to take over.

Golf teachers stress that we should make the pre-shot routine the same for every shot, over approximately the same time frame. Jack Nicklaus takes about 12 seconds. If you can't concentrate for 12 seconds at a time, perhaps you are in the wrong game. Build up a familiarity, a comfort zone, thinking only about the steps needed to make a good shot. Some players, such as Sergio Garcia, who in the past has waggled his club up to 25 times, carry it to extremes. Brian Payne of the Canadian Tour makes 35 to 40 body movements, at times wiggling like a snake.

The following is a list of productive steps. You may want to tinker with this or come up with something that suits your style and personality. Don't worry if a foursome behind you is complaining. Stay focused.

- Assess the situation: your lie, the weather, position to the hole, your choice of club, alignment to the hole.
- Focus on the process, not the potential results.
- Focus on the target you have chosen, not distractions.
- Stand briefly behind the ball, visualizing what you want to happen, not what could happen.
- Align yourself properly to the target; relax and swing confidently.

The pre-shot routine also tells you when to hit the ball. "Have you ever played with someone who stood over the ball for a real long time?" said Harold Sieg, Edinburgh, Minnesota, teaching pro. "You have no idea when they're going to hit it. If they don't have a pre-shot routine, they don't know, either."

One of John Means' players on the 1998 NCAA champion team, the University of Minnesota Gophers, was James McLean, who says you can't alter your routine for a pressure shot. "I hit it the same at any time in a tournament," he said. "When I step over the ball, it's time to pull the trigger."

Small Target vs. Distractions

Many teachers recommend selecting the smallest target possible when focusing, whether it is the flag, or a spot on the green or the fairway. "A golfer's brain performs best when focused on a small, precise target," says sports psychologist Bob Rotella.

Indeed, our biological nature shows us that as our focus narrows, our response becomes more effective, partly due to hormones that affect concentration. Look at the dramatic fight-or-flight response. In it, nature narrows our focus to the threat at hand, putting all its resources behind the defence. Looking intently at a small target, says Gord Chilton, a golf graduate of Slippery Rock (Pennsylvania) College, "takes all the bad things out of play."

The opposite of focusing on a small target is allowing yourself to be sidetracked by larger distractions. And, boy, distractions lurk around the golf course like goblins in a fun house, including all the "self-chatter" going on in your head: "Will my swing hold up?" or "Am I good enough to play with this group?" or "What will my partners think if my game stinks?"

As well, we often bring other distractions with us to the golf course. Your bag and your clubs are the only baggage you should have with you. Abandon your issues from home and work, and don't feel guilty about it. Think of the course as a sanctuary. Life will go on without you for one afternoon. Then, when faced with hazards on the course, don't try to block them out of your mind; that will happen automatically if you are focusing correctly on the target. Instructors recommend focusing on what you want to do rather than what you don't want to happen; the brain responds better to direct, proactive orders.

It is probably best for most amateurs to refrain from adding up their scores as they go from hole to hole. However, most professionals like to know the score if they are in contention late in a tournament or are in danger of missing the cut on Day Two, so they can make some strategy decisions. Others, such as Wendy Doolan of the LPGA, become so absorbed in playing one shot at a time, they deliberately don't look at the leader board. They don't want to get too up or down about the results. "I didn't look at the leader board at No. 17 because I didn't want to confirm my lead and then choke," said Paul Davenport after winning the 2000 TELUS Edmonton Open on the Canadian Tour. When she was at Louisiana State University, Jackie Gallagher-Smith won the school's tournament, partly because she wasn't worrying about the results. She was in charge of keeping her partners' scorecards. "I remember not wanting to write down any of their scores because I didn't want to think about what they were shooting," she said. "I wanted to stay in focus in my own game. When I finished, I didn't even know I'd won because I was so wrapped up in what I was doing."

As amateurs, we can pick up both good and bad behavioural habits from watching pros. In recent years, it seems the pros are become increasingly more irritable with distractions around them. David Duval sometimes walks away from his ball and angrily motions into the crowd to find out who has been making a slight noise when he is entering his pre-shot routine.

On the LPGA Tour, Gail Graham blamed a cell phone for ruining her long putt, then threatened to come into the crowd to take it away from its owner. Scotland's Colin Montgomerie has become known as Rabbit Ears for hearing criticism from the gallery. Ernie Els and Jesper Parnevik have blamed marshals for ruining their concentration. Carlos Franco backed off in disgust at the sound of a Johnny-on-the-Spot closing. And Tiger Woods is also at times sensitive, snapping at those whose cameras shutters click. "From what I've seen, a certain grumpiness pervades on the tour," said Ted Purdy, who qualified for the PGA Tour in 1999.

Before we criticize the pros too harshly, understand that they live in an entirely different environment than amateurs. Pressure to make money is always there and the more pressure you feel, the more susceptible you are to irritability. Pro galleries are growing larger and getting noisier, even heckling on occasion — and in some remote cases, a little drunk. Others are bringing young children to tournaments or sneaking cell phones and cameras onto courses, even though they are banned. At the 2002 Sony Open, a ringing cell phone cost John Cook $288,000, the difference between first and second place.

But some players are simply using noisy fans as an excuse for a lousy shot, says Toronto exercise physiologist Laurie Burns, who works with golfers and officials to help players deal with distractions. They must learn to block out noise through breathing and concentration techniques, just as athletes in other sports do, she said.

Players often react negatively to unnatural noises because for centuries golf has been a sport of etiquette. How dare we break the code of silence? But years ago, amateurs at the Pasatiempo Golf Club near Santa Cruz, California, learned to deal with such

distractions. They had no choice. In an annual event called the "Boo Tournament," players were allowed to spook their opponents with talking and heckling. Interestingly, the average scores turned out to be no higher than in any other tournament at the club. "Knowing that they could expect any trick in the book and some that weren't, and being in no doubt about the intention behind the cajoling, many golfers quickly learned to tune out everything that came their way and focused more completely on each shot," author Timothy Gallwey said.

Perhaps a more difficult chore is to calm what is going on inside your head: the worries, self-doubts, self-consciousness and sometimes overconfidence. The only way to remove these distractions is by clearing your mind and thinking only of the task at hand, the shot. Getting back to the "power of now." This may take practice and many golfers report that taking yoga or meditation classes helps them eventually achieve a better mind-set.

Visualization

Visualization is focusing on what you want to happen and making a mental picture of it *before* it happens. It has been a common self-improvement technique for some time, yet some golfers still think it's hokey, even spooky. (After blowing many chances for victory in 2001, Phil Mickelson in desperation dug out his old college papers on visualization and they helped him.) Really, though, it is something we all do from time to time — just a form of hope and thinking proactively, believing in a sunny outcome. When you focus at the target, you are imagining where the ball will end up. Without this belief, you would likely never break 90.

Most elite golfers have taken this further, with detailed imagery of what their ball will do. A survey revealed that older and better-educated athletes tended to use mental practice more. Psychologists say that the lower parts of our brain and central nervous system cannot distinguish between something that has been vividly imagined and something which has actually occurred. Maxwell Maltz discovered that when an athlete visualized, all the nerves involved in moving the muscles were electrically stimulated, although at a lower than normal level.

Some stunning results have been reported by PGA players. "I rehearsed everything about the shot in my mind before I even picked up the club," said Paul Azinger after his sand shot won the 1993 Memorial Tournament. Peter Jacobsen once used a training technique in which he putted for up to 30 minutes without using a ball, holing one imaginary putt after another, then he went out and won the Colonial National Invitational. "If we train ourselves to imagine positive things, such as consistently making 10-foot putts, we can make real 10-foot putts, as well," Jacobsen said.

Jack Nicklaus describes how he mentally programs each shot: "I never hit a shot, even in practice, without having a very sharp, in-focus picture of it in my head. It's like a colour movie. First I see the ball where I want it to finish, nice and white and sitting up high on the bright green grass. Then the scene quickly changes and I see the ball going there: its path, trajectory and shape, even its behaviour on landing. Then there's a sort of fade-out, and the next scene shows me making the kind of swing that will turn the previous image into reality. Only at the end of this short, private Hollywood spectacular do I select a club and step up to the ball." Nicklaus says that many amateurs neglect this programming. "I believe a few moments of movie-making might work some small miracles in your game. Just make sure your movies show a perfect shot. We don't want any horror films of shots flying into sand or water or out of bounds." Nicklaus makes a good point: Too many golfers are negative or at least doubting in their pre-shot thinking. That's when they hesitate, even choke, leading to tension and a poor swing.

Two-time Masters winner Seve Ballasteros isn't confident until he visualizes. "In order to gain confidence, I must be able to *see* — clearly visualize mentally — a line all the way from my ball to my actual target, both at the start of the setup and, equally importantly, at the end of my routine," he said. "Once everything checks out A-okay, my entire body responds by swinging the club almost reflexively in response to the picture in my mind's eye."

Arnold Palmer says a golfer must be proactive before a shot. "He must say to the ball, 'Go to that spot.'"

Imagery: Emotional Thoughts

Some experts suggest going further in visualization to include sights, sounds, smells and even emotions. This is sometimes referred to as imagery. Bob Phillips, director of the Golf Psychology Training Center in Norcross, Georgia, says that athletes who focus on the strong emotions of a performance are more successful than those who focus only on the images. "Imagery is very helpful in preparing for peak performance and it is actually the emotions in the imagined scene that seem to make the process most effective," he said. "The best way to accomplish this higher level of emotion is to be sure that you step into the image. If you simply see yourself doing the action, you are not really practising the swing or putt and consequently you are not involved with the feeling as deeply as you could be. Make sure you are aware of what you see, hear and smell in the scene." Some people do this naturally, but like everything else in golf, imagery takes some work and self-discipline, especially when doubts or self-pity appear. Sometimes you have to force yourself to go through the process.

A perfect spot for visualization or imagery is the pre-shot routine. "Work hard to develop a mental rehearsal," says Brian Ehrich, a clinical and sport-performance psychologist in Chanhassen, Minnesota. "Visualize the shot you want to make. Imagine a great shot that you made in the past and use all of your senses to return your mind to that shot." Many pros use this technique, including the PGA's Mike Weir, who says, "For a big shot, I flood my mind with memories of good shots I've made in the past."

Some players use imagery in a broader sense. Two-time U.S. Open champion Lee Janzen practises it before a tournament begins. "I set goals for myself, of course, then I see myself doing it once the tournament starts," he said. "I imagine what I'd do when certain situations come up. When they come up, I feel like I've already been there."

FOCUS TIP: KEEP BUSY

Jack Nicklaus says that, among other things, proper focus helps you relax and relieves tension. "Concentration is a fine antidote to anxiety. I have always felt that the sheer intensity Ben Hogan applied to the shot-making specifics was one of his greatest assets. It left no room in his mind for negative thoughts. The busier you can keep yourself with the particulars of shot assessment and execution, the less chance your mind has to dwell on the if-and-but factors that breed anxiety."

"Golf is a spiritual game. It's like Zen."

—Amy Alcott, *winner of* 29 LPGA *tournaments*

CHAPTER 16

ULTIMATE FOCUS:
Looking for Flow

Many golfers report that the ultimate and most enjoyable state of focus is when they get lost in their game, when their endeavours seem so effortless. This experience is a sort of continuing focus, an immersion that can last one hole, several holes or an entire 18. It happens to hackers, to low handicappers, even to pros. The disappointing part is that it doesn't happen very often. Even more frustrating is that most golfers believe they do not have any control over bringing it on. It seems to happen all by itself.

For decades, this has been called getting into the zone. Nowadays, the contemporary catchword for this state is *flow*. I fudge a little by calling it the *flow zone*, but sometimes it defies description by any mortal. Mihaly Csikszentmihalyi, an expert in concentration and professor of management at Claremont Graduate University in Claremont, California, has become world famous for his research on flow and has written several books on the subject. In his book *Flow in Sports*, co-authored by flow researcher Susan A. Jackson, a lecturer at the School of Human Movement Studies at Queensland University of Technology in Australia, Csikszentmihalyi says that flow is a type of focus. "But it's a balance, really, between a total focus and a total release in a way," he said. "You are totally focused, but on the other hand, it is also happening on its own. It is like it is a total automatic process. The things you are saying to yourself throughout the whole performance are automatic in a way. They're the things that you've said to yourself over and over again in training. It is like you are taking all of the good parts of all of your training, and they are happening automatically."

Seeking the Holy Grail of Golf

If choking in golf is a virus, flow is a cure. But it is a cure in progress. Scientists and golf instructors know that it is there, but they struggle to find the formula.

Flow is not only complex, but fleeting. When it comes, which may be only a dozen times over the term of a golfer's life, it is beautiful and more satisfying than scoring low, and yet most often we don't know how we reached the state. Many of the thousands of golfers and other athletes I've interviewed over the years say that you don't find flow, but rather flow finds you. They believe that if you are consciously trying to reach this subconscious state, you will never get there. If you try to immerse yourself, that in itself may become a distraction. Flow, it seems, is a no-think mode.

Perhaps you can do your own little bit of research. If, on one fortunate afternoon, you are able to achieve a flow state on the golf course, go home and try to examine what was in your mind before the round:

- **Maybe** you just set out to have fun that day and didn't concern yourself with the score.
- **Maybe** you were in a good mood and didn't care what happened. That, right there, seems to be one major key to attaining flow: sometimes the less we try, the better we do.
- **Maybe** you had the right blend of partners, who encouraged one another and didn't judge you.
- **Maybe** you had been working on the weaknesses of your game in the previous week or two and let the muscle memory take over.
- **Maybe** you focused your attention on the process of your game and not on the potential results. It's possible you did not even keep score.

Csikszentmihalyi believes that golfers and other athletes cannot summon themselves into the state of flow at will. "Flow does not begin in the mind; it comes from physical or mental performance," he said. "You can't make it happen, but you can invite flow by preparing for greater challenges, removing distractions and learning to focus. It helps to establish a routine. There almost has to be a physical ritual to achieve flow. Some athletes have a certain way of practising, a certain way of tying their shoes before a contest." In this regard, he added, the pre-shot routine is valuable in golf. But training is needed because skill is necessary to reach flow, he added. If the challenge is too great for a golfer's expertise, discouragement can set in.

Steps to the Flow Zone

After much of my own research into peak performance and also into why golfers choke, I believe there are ways you can allow flow to happen more often. Much of this strategy comes before you go out to play and it is a type of subconscious programming.

It would be difficult to start out your day by saying that you are going to get into the zone, or achieve flow. "See you, honey, I'm off to the Public Downs to see Rod Serling in the Twilight Zone." Rather, if you take the following five steps, immersion and flow may follow as a natural consequence. Don't fret if it doesn't work right away. As ironic as it sounds, losing yourself may take effort in the beginning. Prepare well, then forget about everything. Here are the five steps:

- Seek out challenges and golf courses within your reach.
- Program your subconscious with practice on the range, then have faith in your swing.
- Set out to have fun and enjoy the entire experience of the day.
- Don't think so much; lose yourself in the game.
- Focus on the process of golfing, not the score or beating someone or to boost your ego.

Don't expect to reach the flow zone through high arousal or by trying to dominate an opponent or the golf course, many experts say. John Douillard of Boulder, Colorado, teaches professional and amateur athletes and coaches about flow techniques. He says it is hard to achieve by getting pumped up. Instead, you have more of a chance, he said, by being calm, even spiritual in your outlook to a game. "Flow is more related to Eastern philosophies such as Tao and Zen. In ancient cultures, exercise was a piece of a much larger puzzle," Douillard said. "The original Kung Fu masters, for example, spent hours not to master the art of breaking bricks but to unleash their full human potential, to achieve what they called enlightenment."

According to Csikszentmihalyi, flow has more chance of happening if a golfer is not angry and does not let his or her ego come into play, but rather uses the game to improve skills or to meet the challenge that an opponent or a golf course presents. "Competition improves experience only as long as attention is focused primarily on the activity itself," he said. "If extrinsic goals, such as beating the opponent, wanting to impress an audience or obtaining a big professional contract, are what one is concerned about, then competition is likely to become a distraction, rather than an incentive to focus consciousness on what is happening."

Johnny Miller had a flow-zone experience while shooting 63 on the final day to win the 1973 U.S. Open. "I just remember I was very confident and not thinking of the consequences," he recalled. "I was just thinking of fairways and knocking it right at the pin. I didn't play safe golf at all. I played a lot like a little kid would have played." Miller added that reaching the zone is a huge task. "I think it's a lot like a complex recipe for a dish or a pie and if you miss one ingredient, it doesn't taste quite right. In golf, there's a recipe for the zone. I think it is really being in harmony with what you're doing. Wanting to do it, wanting it for the right reasons, not for money or greed or power. And I think love is a secret — if you really love what you're doing and want to share your skills with people watching you and you love the course."

No Think and the Internal Eye

"In every tournament there are a few rounds of super golf; without a doubt they are played subconsciously."

— golf pro Chick Evans Jr.

When it is time for shot-making, it is time to stop thinking. "Anybody can get into the zone playing golf by simply getting out of his or her head," says California teaching pro Debbie Steinbach, who tells her clients to trust their swing and not to care about what might happen.

Whether or not we get into the elusive flow zone, we can do ourselves a great service by thinking about nothing (at the very most one or two swing thoughts) while standing over the ball. In Chapter 2, we discussed the important issue of how much thought processing occurs in the human mind, an average of 66,000 times per day. Of those, 44,000 are negative and often set off our emergency fear system or worry system. "The trouble with me is I think too much," says LPGA legend JoAnne Carner. "I always said you have to be dumb to play good golf."

So what are we to do about this out-of-control thinking? First off, we must become aware of the fact that we think so much. For a short-term remedy, slow, deep breathing can usually help, if we pretend we are letting all the air out of our thoughts. "There go my worries about losing," or "There goes my tension ... *ahhh*." Focusing on breathing or the shot process can distract us from our own thoughts.

But if we don't want our thinking to get out of control in the first place, we must, as Debbie Steinbach says, get out of our head altogether. If we look upon all the activity in our mind as being the product of an internal eye, we may be able to visualize a remedy. Unlike our external eyes, the undisciplined internal eye is not in a socket and it can spin 360 degrees of its own free will, looking for things to create mental images of. When we feel the internal eye taking over, we can use cue words to get control and focus on our golf shot. Try words like "halt!" or "focus!" or "reload!" (Or come up with your own terms.) You've got to control the internal eye or it will control you. Another method is to turn off your internal eye altogether. Remember that golf is a game to be played outdoors on a golf course, not inside your head. If nothing else, playing outside your head relieves the emotional pressure building up in your body. Golf is often too much of a mental game because we allow it to be.

Golf teacher Fred Shoemaker describes this process as becoming "extrospective." "Over the years, I've noticed that enjoyment in golf always shows up when you *disappear*, when your thoughts aren't so much about you and your game," he said. "Most people can't pay attention to what's really happening because there is so much rattling around in their heads. Consider becoming extrospective. Focus your attention on the real things before you: your body, the club, the ball and the course." Shoemaker recommends that, between shots, golfers take notice of everything around them: the colours, the shadows, the curve of the land. "The typical golfer walks stiffly with head down, mulling over the last shot or the next shot, noticing very little."

Exercising between shots is another way to stimulate your consciousness and make yourself three-dimensional, to relieve the pent-up thoughts and pressure. Also, away from the course, some golfers take yoga or meditation classes as a long-term program for quieting the mind and learning to become totally immersed in their game.

"I don't like idle chit-chat."

— Karrie Webb

CHAPTER 17

BETWEEN SHOTS

Years ago when Arnold Palmer was in his prime, I was convinced he had a crush on my then-fiancée, Jennifer. During a round at the Canadian Open at Cherry Hill in Ridgeway, Ontario, Arnie relaxed between his all-or-nothing shots by turning his rugged frame toward the gallery and looking at our faces. More specifically, he looked at Jennifer. Hole after hole! Perhaps it was her floppy, polka-dot hat that caught his eye, or perhaps her striking good looks, but I felt doubly jealous because he wasn't watching me, his biggest fan. *Hey, Arnie, over here!*

Years later, after finally forgiving Arnie, I realize he was ahead of his time in such a technique. The success of your golf round, he knew, may not have everything to do with the shots, but also with what you occupy yourself with between them. A four-and-a-half-hour golf game is actually just minutes of shot-making and the rest is walking, talking, eating a banana and, too often, mulling about things going badly.

"I recommend getting your mind off of golf between shots," says sports psychologist Bob Rotella. "It's easier for most people to concentrate totally for a minute or so at a time, as they execute their shot-making routines. Trying to stay that focused between shots can be too taxing. If you or your partners don't want to talk, try something else. Look at the birds or trees or weeds. Jack Nicklaus used to scan the gallery for pretty girls and joke about setting up his caddy on dates with them." (Jack, please don't use that one if you see Jennifer and me beyond the ropes.)

Because shotmaking can create anxious moments, we must look for ways to loosen up. When the emergency fear system kicks in, it is giving you a physical response to a threat. Exercise is an excellent way to release such nervousness and anxiety. "Golf evolves so slowly and excess energy and anxiety can build with no release," says Jack Raglin, an exercise physiologist at Indiana University. Golfers can release some tension, he said, by walking (no cart) or carrying their own clubs. (On a related note, many golf instructors recommend that amateurs have a period of exercise prior to their round.)

Between shots, why take the game so piously? There's really no need to be solemn and private behind sunglasses like PGA star David Duval. Many pros know the value of staying loose between swings. Lee Trevino jokes with the gallery. Fuzzy Zoeller whistles. Brad Faxon and Lorie Kane sometimes come across the ropes to greet an old friend (in the 1999 New Albany Classic in Ohio, Kane had an old neighbour touch her putter for good luck, then she sank a birdie.) Between strokes, Nancy Lopez brags to her caddy and opponents about her children while Juli Inkster talks about shopping in New York. Mike Weir talks to his caddy about the Toronto Blue Jays. Several LPGA players, including Inkster, sing with their caddies.

"I talk about other things with my caddy — movies we've seen, restaurants we've been to," says Annika Sorenstam. "You just have to find a way to clear your mind. When you get to the ball, then it's time to concentrate."

Grace Park, who often twirls her irons like a baton while walking down the fairway, had fun with her caddy. "We joke around a lot and you'll see us making fun of each other rather than being serious for five hours," she said. "We get serious when we have to, but after we've done with business, we're friends."

Gary Cowan, Canada's amateur golfer of the century, according to the Royal Canadian Golf Association, used to seek out sticks in the fairway and break them one by one as he strolled to find his ball. Tiger Woods sometimes chews gum. Miguel Angel Martin puts a tee in his mouth. A few players smoke (especially cigars on the Champions Tour), but that could create another kind of hazard.

TUNE OUT THE FANS

Tournament golfers aren't always advised to listen to fans between shots. That cost Phil Mickelson the 2001 PGA Championship in Atlanta. On the 16th hole, Mickelson was tied for the lead when he listened to the advice of fans surrounding the green as he faced a 45-foot birdie putt. "A few people behind me in the gallery kept telling me the green was very slow," Mickelson later recalled. "I didn't think it was that slow, but I couldn't block their advice out of my head and I banged the putt (six feet) past the hole." He missed the comeback putt and finished second to David Toms. "I should have trusted my own read of the green."

Your imagination can be a good tool between shots. "You don't have to leave the course to help escape a tense situation," says sports psychologist Patrick J. Cohn. "You can visualize a tranquil scene like a beach or a forest. You can imagine yourself in a familiar setting that is relaxing to you. It is similar to daydreaming, but you have a purpose in mind, which is to take a time out from a stressful situation."

In June 2000, four off-duty firefighters were on the sixth hole at a course in Ajax, Ontario, when a car crashed into a nearby ditch. They rescued him and returned to the fairway to find their golf balls were missing, but the distraction helped Roy Strother re-focus his game and he birdied the next hole.

Most techniques are less dramatic. In their book, *The Eight Traits of Champion Golfers*, Dr. Deborah Graham and Jon Stabler recommend using meditation. "As you walk to your ball, you can use focused meditation by counting your relaxed, deep breaths," they write. "Or you can use awareness meditation by becoming very mentally aware of the feeling of the earth between each step, the shades of green in the landscape, the shapes of clouds or trees, or the feel of the sun or wind on your skin."

Why not enjoy the walk in the park? It would be a shame if, after an entire afternoon of skipping work, after spending $60 on green fees, you came home and the first thing out of your mouth was about your score. And don't forget the chance to strike up a friendship with new partners in your foursome, if only for one afternoon.

Or why not put a new implement into your bag: a ball retriever. My father-in-law has a practical method of killing time — he fishes old balls out of woods and creeks and has never paid for a golf ball in his life. His pals say it is the frugal Dutchman in him, but it gives him something to do between shots.

Australian Brad King did not want to spend all his time between shots with a professional caddy, so he chose his cousin from Perth to carry his bags on the Davidoff Asian Tour. Says King, "He doesn't play golf and knows nothing about it. He is my mate. He keeps me happy, and we chat on the way around. I need someone to talk to me, keep me relaxed and keep my mind on my job. I don't need someone to tell me how far it is or what club to hit. I can do that for myself. Keeping it going for 18 holes is my problem. My mind wanders."

Here is a thought that may sound odd at first: why not combine golf with something like birdwatching or become a minor expert on flora around the courses? Put a small camera in the side pouch of your golf bag and shoot the surroundings as well as your foursome.

Just stay away from polka-dot hats, please.

"There's an involuntary urge ... to shorten the agony."

— Jack Nicklaus

CHAPTER 18

SPECIALTY SHOTS:
First Tee and the Short Game

S pecialty shots, such as putting and hitting off the f-f-f-first tee, can create their own kind of pressure, so they require special attention and focus.

First Shot of the Day

Nowhere is pressure greater and good focus more required than on the first tee. On your drive over to the golf course, your mind will probably jump ahead and worry about what will happen on that first shot of the day, with other golfers waiting for their turn and watching you. "First tee jitters are normal," says Bee Epstein-Shepherd, of Carmel, California, who coaches golfers in mental skills.

Don't worry, she says — things are never as bad as they seem. As a golfer, it can help to recall other potentially stressful moments you have worried about, such as making a speech in front of others, or going to the dentist or the doctor, or taking a test. Once you get to those places, do you ever get the feeling they are usually never as bad as you had anticipated? You might even be annoyed at yourself for wasting time worrying.

Once you arrive at the course, you can do certain things to reduce your fears. One is to warm up physically. It is advisable to play at a course with a practice range or at least a portable tee-and-net gizmo, which allows you to take full swings. "We are embarrassed that we top the ball on the first tee," says Dave Striegel, a sports psychologist in Orlando, Florida. "It doesn't cross our minds that when tour players or skilled amateurs play, they warm up for 45 to 90 minutes and have practised each part of their game and hit that tee shot many times."

Lisa Hackney, the LPGA's rookie of the year in 1997, agrees. "Amateurs are worried about all sorts of things — who they're playing with, who's watching, whether they're going to top it. But most pros are already ready by the first tee because of their preparation. I've practised, I have a strategy and I'm rarin' to go."

Another good pre-round routine recommended by teachers and physiologists is exercise. It's a good idea to exercise before you hit your first shot, or even have a substantial workout or run beforehand. This not only loosens and warms you up, it releases some pent-up tension you might not even know you have. The exercise can ease the muscles tensed by this subconscious fear.

After the exercise and the practice, remember about focus and trusting your swing. Then you will be fine when the starter calls your name. The pre-shot routine will be your friend all day. Vivien Saunders, a British sports coach and former LPGA player, says that confidence, even a swagger, can overcome nervousness. "On the first tee, feel in command in the match even before you tee off," she said. "Don't trudge onto the tee, nervously and apologetically, with suggestions that you are over-awed and honoured to play with your opponent (unless she really is a superstar). Don't utter some drivel about hoping you give her a good game."

If you always get a little scared on tee No. 1, welcome the great Jack Nicklaus to your club. "The big killer on the first tee — for me as much as for you — is tension, both physical and mental," he said. "For me, the ultimate answer to first-tee stress is deliberation. There's an involuntary urge to hurry, to shorten the agony. I never hit any golf shot until I'm ready, but on the first one I always make a conscious effort to be extra deliberate, first in planning the shot, then in setup and finally in swing tempo."

In certain situations, getting pumped up can help you focus. "Think of somebody who makes you mad," says PGA player Notah Begay III (careful of that unpredictable anger, though). "Seriously. Maybe it's your boss. Otherwise, try to gradually pick up your speed in the first half of your downswing. Exercise control on the way back, then try to generate all your speed on the way down."

Many club pros recommend that high handicappers use anything but a driver off the first tee when jitters reign; it is better to employ the longest club that you have confidence in to get the ball into play. Even a five-iron will suffice, if you are not too wrapped up in looking aggressive in front of others. If you are a short hitter, remember there is nothing wrong with a bogey to start the round, but a double- or a triple-bogey could put you in a difficult hole. Betsy King is most scared on the first tee of her own Betsy King Classic because her pride becomes an issue. "The hardest shot for me is the first tee; I'm more nervous at my tournament than I am on the first tee of the U.S. Open."

Whatever weapon you choose, you may want to use one or two swing thoughts to get the day off to a good start: "Slow on the backswing," or "Follow through." A fast backswing or poor follow-through are techniques for calamity.

Epstein-Shepherd tells her students to use mental rehearsal to instruct their subconscious minds before the first shot. "When you tie your shoes, the subconscious moves the muscles in your fingers to create a bow," she said. "In the same way, when you tell yourself to hit a long, straight drive, your subconscious will try to make it happen. If you think about topping or shanking the ball, you are giving bad instructions to your subconscious, which is likely to create actions to match. Ever try to consciously tie your shoelaces? It's faster when you don't think. And when you are fearful and anxious, or think about mechanics, your subconscious does not know what to do — your muscles will tense and your shot will suffer." Epstein-Shepherd also recommends you relax while waiting to tee off by inhaling slowly, gently and deeply to the count of three, then exhaling slowly until the count of five. "As you breathe slowly, your muscles must relax, and as you focus on your count, anxious thoughts leave your head. A relaxed mind and clear head will produce your best shots. Anytime you feel nervous is a good time for breathing exercises."

Visualization should be part of your pre-shot routine. "Visualize a good drive you hit off the first tee in the past on any course," says golf teacher Jim McLean. "Really concentrate, so that you can clearly picture a well-hit accurate drive, and do it over and over. You will alleviate anxiety and the muscles in your body will begin to relax, readying you to make a nice, accelerating golf swing."

And wherever your first ball flies, remember that the first tee is a testing round, not only to see what a good shotmaker you are, but how you handle pressure and embarrassment. Trust your character to survive. So what if you flub it? You might actually perform a service to take the pressure off those watching behind you. If you show that you aren't ashamed if you top the ball, they might not be ashamed, either. Hey, we're all in this nutty game together.

Another problem with putting too much pressure on yourself on the opening shot is that you might believe that if you get off to a rocky start, it will result in a poor round. In reality, though, it is only one shot — if you allow it to be just one shot.

Putting: Terror at Four Feet

Like other aspects of golf, putting has strong elements that are physical, mental and emotional. Most experts agree that putting is the most important aspect of your ability to score. It is also the most susceptible to nerves, because the closer you get to the hole the more you become concerned about finishing off, and also because your wrists, hands and fingers, the parts of your body you use for feel in the short game, are sensitive to your nervous feelings. These are the *small muscles*. When you are very nervous, they may start to shake because your mind-body's emergency fear system diverts blood from your hands and fingers into your upper arms and legs. This makes you ready to fight or run away from a threat (remember our primitive emergency system described in Chapter 2?).

For woods and long irons, it is the *big muscles* of the arms and shoulders that are more dominant in your swing, and they are generally less sensitive to jittery nerves; in fact, they can prosper from the emergency fear system with increased power for long shots. In this regard, it is advisable that you do not get too psyched up around the greens because it will supply extra strength and energy through your emergency fear system. That's okay for your woods and long irons because it enhances your big muscles, but it can make your hands and other small muscles shake. And so emotional calmness is recommended around the greens.

Choking can happen on any shot, but it is more prevalent in putts around four feet in measurement, says 1999 Canadian women's amateur champion Mary Ann Lapointe. "The closer to the hole you get," she says, "the more pressure there is to make it." For Patrick Falvey, a pharmaceutical scientist and a 12-handicapper at the Blue Hill Golf Club in Pearl River, New York, his bout of nerves only appears when he is approaching the green. "I am quite a good chipper in practice, but in an actual round, my arms become like lead weights," he says.

Some pros say you should grip the putter as you would hold a bird in your hand — not hard enough to squeeze the life out of it, and yet hard enough so the bird does not escape.

The correct tension in your grip is vital, according to Morris Hatalsky, a four-time winner on the PGA Tour. "It is important that you milk the putter," he said. "Milking the putter is regripping of the putter until you've got constant grip pressure in both hands. If you monitor that, you will not manipulate that putter head."

Another way to keep your putting stroke smooth is to put less emphasis on the small muscles as you hold the putter. Sam Snead recommends that players develop a style that de-emphasizes too much use of the wrists. "If you use your small muscles and are a wrist putter, I think you are headed right for the yips," he said. A so-called *pure pendulum swing*, with emphasis on the big muscles of the arms and shoulders, is recommended by many teachers to keep the ball on line when shaking may make it go awry.

With the pendulum stroke, you may be able to grip the club more tightly. "The next time you face a three- to six-foot pressure putt, grip the club a little more firmly than normal so you are

NEW STYLES OF PUTTING

For most of the history of golf, putting has been conventional, an extension of the other swings we take during the course of a round. In recent years, though, new putting styles have surfaced and many of them are beneficial in reducing the reliance we have had on the fingers and small muscles or on our dominant hand, especially when we are nervous. Let's review some of the new styles:

- **Cross-handed** — For right handers, the conventional grip is reversed, with the left hand placed low and the right hand higher. Fred Couples, Nick Faldo and the late Payne Stewart have tried it on the PGA Tour, while Karrie Webb, Se Ri Pak and Juli Inkster use it on the LPGA circuit.
- **Long putter** — Held high with the shoulders doing most of the work. The fingers of the right hand are placed across the grip, rather than around it. Used by Scott McCarron.
- **Belly putter** — It's anchored against your gut, taking the hands out of it almost completely. Used by Vijay Singh, Paul Azinger and at one time Colin Montgomerie.
- **Claw grip** — The left hand is held conventionally, but the fingers of the right hand are placed across the grip rather than around it. This is designed to minimize the right hand and its disciples say they are able to make more of a pendulum stroke with the putter. Mark Calcavecchia used the claw because he was suffering from the yips. Tiger Woods has tinkered with it in practice.

more apt to make a pure pendulum stroke," says John Andrisani, a former golf instructor and author of *The Short Game Magic of Tiger Woods*. "The player who is tense over the ball usually has difficulty making a pure pendulum swing ... typically, he or she uses the small muscles of the hands to swing the putter. This makes it difficult to swing the putter on the correct path. To alleviate tension and promote a big-muscle-controlled stroke, hold the putter head slightly off the ground. Practise this new setup position and slowly incorporate it into your on-course routine."

Some PGA players claim that unconventional styles have improved their putting, especially under pressure. When Calcavecchia was in a slump in 2002, he noticed he was starting to twitch over short putts, so he went to the claw grip, which Chris DiMarco had used to win the Phoenix Open that year. "It felt weird at first, but I kept practising and soon I just had this big old grin on my face," said Calcavecchia, who improved his scoring.

Also that year, Kevin Sutherland was still without his first win after 183 PGA Tour starts. When he checked the tour's putting stats, he noticed that DiMarco and Calcavecchia had climbed to first and second place, respectively. Both had been having putting woes prior to switching to the claw. "Man," Sutherland said to himself, "maybe there's something to that." He decided to try it and in his second event, his long losing skid ended as he captured the Match Play Championship. Also in 2002, David Peoples used the claw grip to tie for second at the Touchstone Tucson Open, his best finish since 1992.

Many pros believe that putting cross-handed reduces the chances of choking. "My data shows most tour players miss pressure putts to the left," says putting guru Dave Pelz, an advocate of the cross-hand. "When golfers pull it, they often say they choked. Players miss fewer putts to the left when putting with the left hand low." (Of course, there may be other technical factors involved in this complicated issue.)

But others don't believe in such unconventional styles. "I hope they all go cross-handed because it means they all have a little doubt in their minds," Davis Love III said. Love should know. He was known as a golfer who tended to choke under pressure before he won the 1997 PGA Championship.

Former PGA player Jim Nelford, now a CTV announcer, believes the unconventional grips are "against the spirit of the game. Sure, they help guys with choking, but that's all part of the game," he said. "I think those putting styles should be banned."

If you have problems on the greens and with choking, perhaps you should try one of the unusual methods, but remember that good putting under pressure also involves the mental and emotional issues addressed in this book.

Two-time Masters winner Bernhard Langer has used the cross-handed style, and later in his career he has tried the belly putter. But Langer says you can lower your putting average by lowering your expectations and trying to manage your pressure. As a youngster on the European Tour in 1976, Langer suffered serious putting problems, partly from financial pressure. "I think part of the problem was that I put too much pressure on myself," he said. "I did not have much money and I wanted to succeed quickly. I was lodging in some terrible places, the cheapest I could find. I didn't want to spend much money on food and I couldn't afford a caddy."

Golf teacher David Leadbetter recommends the use of visualization around the greens. "A confident player with a good short game works purely on feel and visualization, and all he sees is success." Visualization and intense focus seem more effective when you have a small target. In driving and fairway play, your target is not as precise, but up close, you can focus on the flag or the hole. In your mind's eye, you can see the ball landing next to the pin or going into the hole quite nicely.

For chipping, Tiger Woods recommends that you visualize your shot before choosing your club. "I pick a spot on the green where I want the ball to land and visualize the ball's flight and roll. That determines my club selection. I will chip with anything from a lob wedge to a three-wood. If I have plenty of room to work with, I might hit a bump-and-run with an eight-iron. If I need to land the ball softly with less roll, I might use a sand wedge.

Many golfers get into trouble when their putting routine speeds up, a common sign of tension. Relaxing and focusing properly are keys to slowing down and gaining control. Although it is generally advised to take your time with a putt, too much dallying can be fatal, as happened with Doug Sanders in the 1970 British Open, who froze over a short putt before missing it on the 72nd hole. "Don't wait or freeze over the ball. The less time to think, the better," says Leadbetter. "Putting is basically all confidence ... practise getting accustomed to knocking the ball into the back of the cup."

As in other areas of golf, confidence and trust are vital steps to successful putting. One of the world's best ever with the narrow blade, four-time British Open champion Bobby Locke, would never make a stroke with doubt. "Hitting a putt in doubt is fatal in most cases," he said.

For further discussion on focus, see Chapter 15.

PUTTING TIP: REBUILD THE STROKE

If you are unhappy with your putting stroke, especially under pressure, read how to rebuild your stroke in *Dave Pelz's Putting Bible*. Here are Dave's recommendations for solving the yips.

- Don't putt to the hole while you rebuild your stroke (allowing you to focus on the stroke and not the results).
- Examine your stroke and find weaknesses.
- Design a practice regimen and stay with it at least six months.
- Make 20,000 good strokes to form a habit of your new stroke.
- Test your stroke on the course and keep the faith.

STRATEGY NO. 4:
MANAGING YOUR EMOTIONAL CHEMISTRY

This section focuses on what to do when you get too nervous or when lousy things happen on the golf course. Ever notice how those two things often go together? How you react to both is a key to success and enjoyment.

If there is a quick-fix section in this book, this is it. Simply put, if we get too aroused (or under-aroused), we need to do one of two things: change our emotional chemistry so that we are back in control, or focus the feelings of fear into our shot.

But before we deliver any techniques on what to do when we feel too much pressure, we need to revisit some of the ideas of Section I. We need to become aware of how we are feeling and what those feelings are doing to our golf game. That will be the focus of Chapter 19.

Then we must decide what to do with our tension or our excitedness; we can change our emotional chemistry, either by calming ourselves (as discussed in Chapter 20) or remaining pumped up and in control at this higher level of alertness (see Chapter 21). In Chapter 22, we will cover the tricky and yet often effective technique of focusing our fear energy into our shot.

Chapter 23 encourages golfers to fight through physical and emotional problems by becoming "grinders."

"The great mind-players are those who never let themselves get too excited when things go in their favour or depressed when things work against them."

— golf teacher Jim McLean

CHAPTER 19

IDENTIFYING AND CHANGING YOUR FEELINGS

Ohne of the main points of this book is that it is best to keep an optimal level of arousal — an even keel — whenever you play golf. In any activity that lasts five hours or more, especially a demanding one such as golf, we cannot afford to get too psyched up or our performance and our enjoyment will suffer. We want to remain relatively calm and relaxed and yet we want our skills to be working at an efficient level.

Robert Thayer, an expert on moods, says it is best to seek a state of mind and emotional chemistry that will last us for hours, a state he calls "calm energy." While in this state, your heart rate, metabolism and respiration rate are relatively high and you are focused, but you feel no sense of urgency, just a quiet and relaxed attention. You might describe it as feeling energetic and confident.

Do not despair if you are in a state of optimal arousal (or calm energy) and you suddenly get tense or aroused. In fact, practically every time you go out to play golf, your physiological arousal levels will probably go up or fluctuate. That is a normal reaction when people engage in an activity with other people, especially during competition, and especially in a game as challenging as golf. Your emergency fear system will kick in quite often, usually at low levels, but enough to influence your skills.

So do not panic. "If you feel excited, pumped or even fearful, accept the feelings as normal," says sports psychologist Terry Orlick of Ottawa. "It is part of the natural rush that comes with putting yourself or your performance on the line. Many performers even miss the feeling when they leave their performance domain."

We need to identify when our arousal levels get high (or low) enough to hurt our game, then know how to change our emotional chemistry to the desired level. Arousal levels will likely be higher on the golf course than on the driving range because of the challenge of the course, other people watching and our own expectations to score well. In certain situations with certain partners, you can get defensive and more aroused. But you must learn to identify these feelings and control your arousal levels or they will control you. "Before you can master competitive pressure and consistently get to an optimal arousal level, you must have an awareness of what under- and over-arousal look and feel like," says Alan S. Goldberg, the director of Competitive Advantage, a sports consulting firm in Amherst, Massachusetts. "If you miss the early-warning signs of excessive arousal, you may not have time to do anything constructive about it once the performance begins. Your ability to stay cool in the clutch depends on how well you can learn to read your physiological signals."

Says 1999 European Ryder Cup captain Mark James, "Nerves? It's something you have to be aware of at the time it's hitting you. If it happens and you don't know it's happening, you're in trouble."

What often separates elite golfers from the rest is that they are able to read their pre-performance nervousness and they can change its level as needed, Goldberg said, whether that is having to get psyched when they are under-aroused or calm when they are too keyed up. You have to know yourself like you know your golf game and your golf course.

"I have to acknowledge my nerves and get my emotions out on the table," says LPGA player Jill McGill. Another LPGA player, Joan Pitcock, adds, "There is definitely a tremendous amount of pressure I feel out there. I think I recognize it instead of ignoring it. I wouldn't say I embrace it, but it would be ridiculous to say that there's no pressure."

But even many professionals have poor arousal awareness, according to veteran LPGA and PGA caddy Tom Hanson, who sometimes takes it upon himself to make up for their lack of education. In the 1993 U.S. Women's Open at Crooked Stick Golf Club in Carmel, Indiana, Hanson was caddying for Lauri Merten, who was tied for the lead on the final tee. "I recognized she was pumped up because she normally hit her drive 220 [yards] and she hit it 250," he said. "But I don't think Lauri understood this. On her second shot, she would normally have used a five-iron, but deep down, I knew she was pumped, so I told her she had a wind behind her and that she should use a six-iron." Merten put the shot to within three feet of the flag and won the championship.

In 1998 on the PGA Tour, Len Mattiace had a chance to win the Players Championship on the TPC at Sawgrass in Ponte Vedra Beach, Florida, his home course. On the 71st hole of the tournament, he tried to lay up before a water hazard, as he often did in practice when his arousal levels were lower. Tom Hanson said, "But he was pumped and his nine-iron went into the water. A lot of players don't hit the ball as far when the pressure isn't on."

AROUSAL SIGNS

Signs that you may be over-aroused (for the technical edicts of this, see Chapter 4):

- gripping the club too tightly
- swinging too quickly
- tempo is disrupted
- problems focusing or with course management
- fast heartbeat
- shallow breathing
- butterflies in your stomach
- trembling
- dry mouth
- walking pace is too fast
- feeling "hyper"
- sweating

Signs that you may be under-aroused:

- loss of clubhead speed
- loss of game tempo
- loss of interest in a pre-shot routine or lining up putts properly
- loss of focus
- lethargy or fatigue
- heaviness in legs and arms
- lack of killer instinct
- overconfidence

Optimal Arousal Levels for Various Activities

The following is subjective, but gives us a general idea of the optimal or manageable arousal levels for various activities. I've put this together after interviewing many athletes, psychologists, coaches and motivation researchers. Many golf instructors believe you can raise your optimal levels by constantly practising and playing under pressure, allowing you to take advantage of the powers of such "fear energy."

5 (extremely excited)	Life-or-death situations
4 (somewhat excited)	Explosion sports (football blocking and tackling, sprinting, golf driving)
3 (aroused but not excited)	Acting, public speaking (at least to start a session)
2 (somewhat aroused)	Golf short game, bowling, typing to deadline
1 (slightly aroused)	Painting a picture, between shots in golf

If you can't make a proper assessment of your arousal levels, ask others in your group if your backswing is too fast or if you are exhibiting arousal signs. "I had to rely on my caddy for this on Sundays," says Sandra Post, an eight-time LPGA winner. "I didn't realize how high I was getting and how I was rushing from one shot to the next. I told him to grab me and pull me back when I did that," she said.

Another step in dealing with tension's effect on your game is to identify which areas of your body get tense most often. Is it your shoulders? Neck? Hands? Pressure and fear often reveal themselves in certain areas of your body. Identify if there is tightness in your swing. "Swing and see if you notice any over-tightness, any lack of fluidity, or any forcing," says golf author W. Timothy Gallwey. "If you have played a good deal of golf, patterns of over-tightness may have become so ingrained in your swing that it is hard to notice them." Just identifying this can relax you, but Gallwey also offers an exercise to try on the practice tee: Hum to yourself while you swing. "I found I could actually hear the tightness of my swing in the sound," he said. In the backswing, the humming would be smooth, "but during the change of direction my voice would become strained and at contact (with the ball) my throat would constrict and the humming would increase in volume, in pitch and, most noticeably, in tightness. Sometimes when I really went after the ball, the hum would stop after contact and I would notice that I had also cut off my follow-through." With humming you can expose over-tightness you are not aware of.

If you are having problems identifying your tension and arousal levels, get feedback from your golfing partners.

Use It or Defuse It

Once you have established that you are over-aroused (we become under-aroused at golf much less frequently), your emergency fear system has pumped out a bunch of powerful hormones to meet what you perceive as a threat. In a moment's notice, you have two choices: defuse the feelings of fear or turn them into extra resources. I want to emphasize this once more: once you have gone above your optimal level of arousal and become too nervous, there are basically two ways to deal with it effectively:

- Change your emotional chemistry, either by defusing the fear with techniques such as deep breathing, self-talk, tighter focus, visualization and pre-shot routines (see Chapter 20), or by getting pumped up but in control at higher levels of arousal (see Chapter 21).
- Redirect the nervous emotions into the shot (see Chapter 22).

Your decision may depend on your skill and your experience under pressure. Highly competent performers can usually stand a higher arousal level. Everyone has different arousal levels, depending on personality, genes and life experience. It is up to you to decide what your optimal level of arousal is; in other words, at what level of arousal you function the best. Levels will fluctuate during the course of a round, but I'm talking about the overall emotional set for the 18 holes, finding your comfort zone somewhere between assertiveness and relaxation.

Different types of shots can require different arousal levels. For instance, you may want to get a little more pumped than usual with your driver or other woods, but not as much with your short game or putting. Relaxation and a light touch are keys on the greens, whereas *grip it and rip it* may be the mindset for some on the tee. Again, it's a matter of what works for you. Tiger Woods says he deals with his nervousness differently on each shot. "Sometimes I take a deep breath; sometimes I step up my breathing for a big shot. Sometimes I have to slow down and sometimes I speed myself up. You've got to do what your body wants to do inside and just trust it ... I'm glad when I feel nervous. If I'm not nervous, I'm not caring enough."

Changing Emotional Chemistry

If you are too nervous, too enveloped in the emotion of fear on the golf course, it means that too much adrenaline and other hormones are pumping through your system, negatively affecting your muscles, your technique and your thinking. You need to change this chemistry by changing your emotion, or at least by bringing your fear to optimal, manageable levels. The linking of emotions may be more natural than we think. South Carolina psychiatrist Mark George revealed through a study that many emotions are more closely linked than previously thought, even happiness and sadness. "It's not one side up or down. Many of our emotions are bittersweet," he said.

Changing your emotional chemistry is easier than you probably imagine. It can be accomplished through deep breathing, deep focus or by changing your thinking. Although we still have much to learn about emotions, we do know that many, if not most of them are triggered by our own thoughts. While thoughts seem intangible, they are among the most powerful things in the world, capable of igniting strong action and change. Merely thinking about something can alter your mood or arouse you physically, sexually or spiritually. Through our thinking, our mind-body chemistry changes all the time, whether we are at work, watching a professional golf tournament on TV or listening to music. Simple thoughts can rapidly alter our emotional chemistry through the limbic system in the centre of the brain, sometimes referred to as the emotional brain. As soon as the system receives a signal (a thought), the emotional response time can be as little as 12 one-thousandths of *one second*. In a blink of an eye, our emotion can change from fear to anger, or from anger to joy. These neural messages motivate physiological changes as powerful hormones are released throughout the mind-body. At the movies, you can be frightened one second, with tingles shooting up and down your spine, laughing heartily the next and then misty-eyed on your way out. And all through the illusions created by light and sound in a theatre! The same thing can occur while watching a professional golf tournament; your excitement levels can rise and fall, along with those of your favourite golfer.

You don't have to be watching someone or something else, however — you can create changes through the use of a computer as sophisticated as any scenario created in Hollywood: your brain, simply by means of your thought processes. In fact, stress expert James E. Loehr calls the summoning of emotions on command "acting,"comparing it to Hollywood; he's been teaching it for years to the world's elite athletes and corporate warriors. "The on switch for an emotion can be fully activated regardless of whether it fits reality as judged by the rational brain," he said. "And once the switch is pulled and the emotion takes hold, the feelings we experience simply confirm that the underlying physiological mechanisms have been activated. What we feel when we are nervous, anxious, angry, or joyous are the mental and physical consequences of highly specific hormonal surges."

Let's try a little exercise. To show how simple thoughts can change your emotions and your chemistry, consider these ideas and think them through a little:

- Pretend someone at your golf club has criticized you unfairly.
- Pretend you have just discovered you have a serious injury to end your golf season.
- If you let these thoughts develop to potential consequences, don't you feel irritated mentally and physically? Nothing has really happened, you just imagined that it did. Now let's imagine some better scenarios:
- Pretend a groundswell of the membership has encouraged you to become club president.
- Pretend that cute golfer you've noticed before is seeking a twosome with you.

Don't you suddenly feel on top of the world? You may have done nothing to deserve these accolades, but you *think* you have gained them. Now, let's reverse both of these scenarios. Try thinking that your serious injury was wrongly diagnosed by your quack physiotherapist. You're okay! You will be back on the links next week. Wow, doesn't relief feel good? And now, you discover that the guy at the clubhouse was criticizing you because he was having a bad day. Whew, it wasn't about you after all. It wasn't personal. Feel that warm physical chemistry sweep through you. Feel the tension in your shoulders or the knot in your stomach dissipating.

Let's keep going. Uh-oh, the membership didn't really want you in as president; they just wanted that jerk incumbent out of there. And the cute golfer —was using you to get the club pro jealous. Don't you suddenly feel down a little? That's natural, even if this whole game is in your head. But this exercise reveals that our mind-body can react to simple thoughts or fantasies much the same as it does to reality. Many psychologists and biochemists believe the autonomic nervous system can't tell the difference between a real or perceived threat or joy. The adrenaline and the endorphins start flowing anyway, although not quite in the same proportion as they do in real life.

On the golf course, if you feel too much tension or frustration or if your concentration is frazzled, it may mean you are too much in the emotion of fear and you need a change of emotional chemistry. A healthy, optimal dose of fear can be a good thing, but not in large amounts. Fear can pump too much adrenaline and cortisol throughout your system and you might freeze or your skills might "choke." So you must change your mindset to get out of the fear mode into a more positive frame of mind and subsequently into a more proactive emotional chemistry.

On and off the golf course, even a small dose of fear often feels uncomfortable and negative, largely because we have not learned to deal with fear in any avenue of our lives. To recruit fear as a proactive force, we need to make it seem like an ally. We can do this by embracing it with another less threatening emotion — such as excitement, levity, joy and even (gulp) anger. These feelings motivate us and get us moving forward, not only mentally, but physiologically. We must combine fear with action to get it into a productive mode.

Over the next three chapters, we will look more closely at changing our emotions and our chemistry.

"Overcoming nerves is the key to scoring well."

— *Karrie Webb*

CHAPTER 20

CHANGING CHEMISTRY:
Coming Down

F acing a shot while we are under- or over-aroused, we must decide quickly which of two paths to take: do we want to change our emotional chemistry (to calm down or get pumped up), or do we want to channel the aroused emotions into our shot? That is your decision to make, depending on the situation, your genetic makeup and your experience.

As a general rule, relaxation is the best state of mind and body for a golf round. In other words, most of the time when aroused, we probably need to come back down to earth, to tell our emergency fear system to back off. Golf cannot be played effectively, or enjoyably, at high levels of arousal, at least not over 18 holes. Getting pumped up can work at selected moments during a competitive match, but what is the point of always playing under pressure to score well if you don't enjoy the round at the end of the day?

Club pros, teachers and psychologists say it's best to try to keep an even keel so that the arousal hormones don't get to unmanageable levels. Amateur great Bobby Jones used to say that relaxation can compensate for a bad golf swing. "It is truly amazing how far we can go if we can only keep from tightening up," said Jones, who played best when he had inner peace. Relaxing decreases heart rate, blood pressure and respiration, and is often accompanied by slower brain wave activity and heightened production of the hormone endorphin, which combats pain and tension and promotes well-being.

For most of us on the golf course, relaxing probably means having to come down slightly, for the overall round or its more tense moments. If you are too tense or too pumped, there are some proven natural strategies to get you back in focus, back into *optimal arousal*. One of them is to slow down your thinking and your movement. Nice and slow, see. Teachers of many elite players even recommend they be deliberately slow in getting out of bed in the morning and in everything they do before competition, setting a relaxed tone for the day. On his way to blitzing the rest of the field in the 2000 U.S. Open, Tiger Woods reported feeling tranquil and calm, despite stormy weather conditions at Pebble Beach.

Strategies for relaxing and coming down tend to be individualistic, from the use of breathing techniques to music to keeping the game in perspective. Manny Zerman, who has played on the PGA, European, Nike and Canadian Tours, uses humour and a personal calming technique to soothe himself. Whenever he feels too nervous, he stops and counts down from five to one and finds it helps slow down his backswing.

TV broadcaster Johnny Miller advises amateurs to loosen up and be aware that, under pressure, they may be gripping the club too tightly. "Only one golfer in a thousand grips the club lightly enough," he said.

Amateur golfer Richard Douglas has gone out of his way to improve his mental game. He sent me an e-mail saying he had been having problems with his nerves acting up under the gun. "It really ticks me off when it happens, which is pretty well every time I'm putting under pressure," he said. "The pressure is always there and fear gets in the way of clear thinking on the greens. I hate fear, but I cannot help but deal with it no matter how poor or embarrassed I feel." After recognizing his problem, Douglas made a concerted effort to slow down, to put less importance on the shot and to relax with his putter, to the point of sometimes getting sleepy. "I am starting to yawn over the ball. This is pretty

---

DANGERS OF ELATION

It is not just poor play or frustration that causes us to get over-aroused. Sometimes the reverse is true. Too much happiness can be just as destructive to your swing. Ask a famous astronaut — we can put a man on the moon, yet we can't seem to calm down and relax when things are going well. During his 1971 moon landing, astronaut Alan Shepard hit a golf ball more than 200 yards with a six-iron in the rare atmosphere. "I was so excited, I swung harder on the second one, which I shanked about 40 yards into a nearby crater," he recalled.

Elation is trouble back on earth, as well. "When I get excited, I don't play very well," says LPGA player Jeong Jang. "I try to subside my excitement."

Bobby Jones said that elation can also scuttle focus. "The most dangerous spot, where the cords of concentration are most likely to snap, comes while everything is going smoothly; when the hold upon concentration is a bit weak, anyway, there is nothing like prosperity to sever the connection."

cool," he said. Continued good luck, Richard, but, of course, there is a fine line between being relaxed and losing interest.

(PGA player Mac O'Grady said some players on tour had such problems with hypertension, they were using beta-blockers, drugs that slows a person's heart rate, allowing a calmer disposition and a smoother swing. But the PGA denied his claim. Beta-blockers are not only discouraged by the tour, they could disrupt a person's chemistry enough to be unhealthy in certain situations.)

Always seek thoughts that bring us to calmness and a neutral state, especially when you have become frustrated or tense. When we feel funky, let's try to shut down our negative thoughts and emotions for a brief period and let relaxation have a chance to set in. But going from the tension of fear to complete serenity by simply turning off all thoughts is easier said than done. It might be easier to force ourselves to *think* of serenity, perhaps with a phrase like "serenity now" (*Seinfeld* buffs might remember that one).

Or perhaps for a few moments we can force ourselves to think of a safe, quiet place we would like to be, away from the pressure: a sandy beach or back in the clubhouse, downing a pint of beer.

Breathing

Almost every good golfer knows that proper deep breathing can reduce anxiety and tension, but it's easy to forget when we are focusing on our score. Again, awareness and discipline must come into play when you are in the heat of the moment. Stop the action and remember to breathe. To drive home the point, talk out loud to yourself. Not only does it add oxygen to your over-working emergency fear system, it forces you to take your mind off your problems and do another activity for a moment. That alone can help get you back on track. When your breathing gets too fast, it can affect your swing, Sam Snead said. "I was always aware of my breathing. When it got shallow and fast, I knew I needed to slow down," he said. "The more you are in tune with your thinking and with what your body is doing, the better you are able to control your swing. This sensitivity that I had to what I was feeling and thinking helped me perform better."

Sometimes it takes focus to get you back on track, to bring you down, says sports psychologist Terry Orlick. "Relaxation is all about controlling focus. Your focus controls your intensity, relaxation and performance. Get your focus in the right place and everything else will be in the right place." He suggests you practise a one-breath relaxation: take a deep breath with long, slow inhalation, followed by a long, slow exhalation. As you breathe out, think "relax" and let your shoulders relax.

In the 1924 U.S. Amateur, Bobby Jones rode to the title by focusing on reducing his heart rate and his breathing before he putted.

In the 1963 PGA Championship, Jack Nicklaus said he had "a sudden attack of nerves" while facing a four-foot putt on the 72nd hole, "but I took my time, along with some deep breaths, and somehow squeezed the ball into the hole for a 68 and a two-shot victory."

It may take some practice to breathe properly, first in a relaxed situation, then under pressure: breathe slowly and deeply through your lower stomach, then slowly exhale, focusing all the while on your breathing technique, with shoulders relaxed, mouth closed. To decrease tension, some players use *diaphragmatic breathing*, using the abdominal muscles to extend the abdomen upon inhaling, allowing oxygen to enter the lungs. During the exhale, the abdominal muscles are contracted, forcing the air out of the lungs.

Former world champion gymnast and college professor Dan Millman says there is a strong link between breathing, your emotional state and meditation. In his book, *The Inner Athletes*, Millman writes: "Breath awareness and discipline were central to the teachings of the most ancient spiritual traditions. Yogis, Zen masters and martial artists have all placed great emphasis on breathing properly. The one unifying link between mind and body is breath. Meditation deals with the mind but could also be called a physical relaxation exercise. Relaxation exercises, in turn, deal with the body but could also be called meditation exercises. Both body and mind are intimately related to the emotions through awareness of breath. The various approaches to well-being demonstrate the intimate relationship of the three centres: physical, mental and emotional. Meditation practices centre around insight and release of thought. As thoughts are released, emotions flow naturally and the body relaxes. As the body relaxes, the mind tends to become quiet as well, and the emotions open up."

EMOTIONS TIP: THE 60-SECOND MEDITATION

(From *Golf, The Winner's Way* by Richard Behrens)

This meditation technique can be used between shots to bring serenity and clarity to the mind.

- Stop your thoughts and clear your mind by exhaling (through the nose) as much air as you can. Then hold your breath a few seconds. You will notice that all your thoughts disappear.
- Begin to breathe in through your nose, very slowly. Follow your breath as it enters your body. Allow that breath to fill your body as if your entire body were hollow.
- Exhale and follow your breath as it leaves your body.
- Continue this exercise until you reach your ball.

Exercising

Exercising before or during a round is a great way to relieve anxiety and tension and to focus on something other than your swing. Stretching your muscles brings more oxygen to them and loosens them up for the shot.

To relax a tense muscle, it is a good idea to make it even more tense, without straining it, then release it. Do this for 10 seconds with each tense muscle: 10 seconds of tight, then release, while exhaling. Feel the anxiety dissipate. The tension might be in your shoulders or your hands. If it is in your hands, deliberately grip the club too tightly, then release.

Decades ago, my physical education coach, Del Davidson, taught me a method that still holds up today: Imagine your muscles as tight ropes, then release them slowly, one at a time. When you have a moment alone, you can do this exercise all over your body by tensing the "ropes," then relaxing.

Two Smiles: On Your Ball and Your Face

"The golf course is a much happier place to be when you're having fun."
— Barry Lane of the European PGA Tour

Humour lubricates your golf game, encouraging a balanced emotional chemistry. It is the natural enemy of too much fear. A laugh (or even a smile) during tense moments automatically releases the hormone endorphin, which eases psychological and physical pain and can loosen your swing. Just try to get tense when you're smiling. As well, laughing lowers blood pressure, forces you to breathe, generally relaxes you and tends to boost spiritual happiness.

Socially, a chuckle at your own expense can make you a hit with your foursome. And perhaps more importantly for most of us, a good guffaw during four hours of intensity can remind us the game should be fun. Hey, that's a novel idea!

Laughter on the links is crucial, says former Southwest Missouri State player Dave Hemstad, now a stand-up comic at golf and business events, "because golf is such a humbling game. You can't take it too seriously; so many things can go wrong." During the 2000 Toronto Star Amateur (Greater Toronto Area Championship), defending champion Hemstad got so pleased about being told he was being hired for a gig, he chuckled and immediately sank a 30-foot putt to make the cut.

The greats know the value of a well-timed guffaw, especially in professional golf with its pressure and premium on tight focus. PGA player John Daly says he is sharper when he can giggle down the fairways. "The more giggles I get, the looser I am, and the better I play." Lee Trevino, Chi Chi Rodriguez and Fuzzy Zoeller have become comics with clubs. "I don't fear death, but I sure do hate those three-footers for par," Rodriguez says.

Sweden's Jesper Parnevik wears outrageous pink pants, helping himself and his opponents keep perspective on Sundays. In the 2000 Nissan Open, Kirk Triplett partly credited Parnevik's clothes with helping him win his first tournament in 265 tries. "I was feeling queasy on the back nine (in the final round), then I looked at Jesper's trousers and suddenly I felt better."

But there is less levity in pro golf than there used to be, says Daly. "Golf has really become a big business and many of the guys are very serious." Sometimes you have to let your personality out, as did Japan's Shigeki Maruyama, who celebrated his win at the 2002 Byron Nelson Classic by wearing a cowboy hat. "I was born like ... this is my personality," he smiled. "If I could speak English, I could make you laugh harder."

Golf can be wacky , with more things to laugh at than hazards. Twice I've broken rental five-irons, their heads flying farther than my shot, although one clubhouse attendant in England didn't see humour in it when I returned the bag. Silly bugger.

My late uncle, Gordon Stuart, was a lightning rod for trouble — over the years, he got hit in the back and the groin with other people's shots and another time a red-winged blackbird would not let him putt out, screaming down upon him, apparently to protect her young in a nearby tree. Gordon always found time to laugh about his follies and I respected him for it.

Notah Begay III had a troubling time early in his 2000 PGA season with a drunk driving conviction, but he rallied for two victories, including one at the FedEx St. Jude Classic, partly because of joking from his caddy, younger brother Clint, who does not help with yardages or read most putts. "I'm having much more fun lately," Notah said.

"We tend to get too serious on the golf course," says PGA veteran Peter Jacobsen. "We've got to try to laugh at ourselves or the conditions. It's not as if someone has pictures of farm animals to blackmail us with."

Former U.S. President Gerald Ford loved golf, but spectators who lined his pro-ams scattered in fear of his tee shots. "I know I'm getting better at golf," he mused, "because I'm hitting fewer spectators."

The internet is loaded with golf humour, such as Jack 'n' Tracy's Baaaaaad Golf Page, set up by a husband and wife who are members of the Wedgewood Country Club near Cabool, Michigan. They write, "A golfer named Joe was paired with a good player and anxious to get some free advice. Hitting first, he swung awkwardly and topped the ball. 'Do you see anything I can correct?' Joe said. His partner responded: 'I see you're standing too close to the ball — after you hit it.'"

We need levity in this game because it is so precise and often unforgiving. Knowing that others will make bogeys might lighten the load. "I'm just trying to have fun," said Tom Byrum while contending for the lead at the 1999 Michelob Championship at Kingsmill. "There's going to be mistakes when the course is playing tough. Don't let them slow you down or get too upset about a bogey here or there. Other guys are making them."

After being hit by lightning in a tournament, Trevino quipped, "I should have held up a one-iron. Not even God can hit a one-iron."

Even super-intense Nick Faldo has learned that loosening up can help his game, as he did while clowning for the TV cameras

while finishing seventh in the 2000 U.S. Open, his best performance in a major in five years.

When a smile suddenly appears on your Titleist, you need to
balance it out with one on your face. When you get too serious
about lowering your score, remember that perfectionism is the
fear of being human. That may have been part of the reason
England's Barry Lane went into a long victory drought on the
European PGA Tour after winning $1 million in the 1995 Andersen
Consulting World Championship of Golf. He credited his wife,
Stephanie, with pointing out that he was becoming too serious.
He made the adjustments that resulted in an improved performance in 2000. "Steph's been telling me for a couple of years to
enjoy my golf," he said. "Play with a smile and that's exactly what
I've done and what a difference. I want to keep on smiling in the
world. Or at least the golf course is a much happier place to be
when you are having fun."

Music to Soothe the Savage Game

Music is one of those reversible intangibles. You can use it to
come down, to get psyched or to keep an even keel, depending
on the type you use.

When Dale Eggeling was brought into the media interview
room at the 2000 Wegmans Rochester International tournament,
she was asked how she makes herself calm when she gets nervous
on the golf course. "I go someplace in my head," she said sheep-
ishly. "It's my little secret, just something I've worked through
that works for me." Later when pressed about it, the 24-year LPGA
veteran said that sometimes she plays songs in her head, "a different song every week, usually something snappy with a beat."

Although some players are reluctant to discuss these intimacies, music can be a soothing, even inspirational force for golfers and can keep them at an optimal level of arousal and rhythm for periods of time. For a game that relies heavily on focus and motivation, music is a natural companion. And it has been proven to raise an athlete's brain levels of the natural drugs endorphin and serotonin, generally associated with calmness, as well as self-esteem and confidence.

Different sporting activities usually require different types of music. According to music therapist Roberta Wigle, heavy rock music can be particularly effective for athletes who have minor injuries, because it masks pain. Fast music is generally less effective for sports and activities that feature spontaneous creativity and thinking and more effective for sports with repetitive moves, such as bowling, says clinical psychiatrist Anthony Storr of Oxford, England, author of *Music and the Mind*.

Golf is harder to categorize because of the various skills required and it may be that you should choose the speed and type of music that work for you. Late PGA legend Sam Snead said music and golf were made for one another. "Golf is all about rhythm and timing. I would love to play golf with music playing over a loudspeaker," he said. "That's where the rhythm and timing come in — it's one, two, three. My swing feels as if it is slow going back and slow starting down, then gradually picks up speed until I get that pop! At impact, it's one, two, three. When I'm playing well, I just feel — how did that old radio-show host put it? I just swing and sway with Sammy Kaye." According to Slammin' Sammy (Snead), you should choose something slow to play in your head. "A waltz is better than a fox-trot. Of course, a lot of the younger people out there might not even know what a waltz is."

For four decades in golf, Larry Gilbert, a member of the Kentucky Golf Hall of Fame, listened to soft, popular music before a round, "usually Barbra Streisand, Sammy Davis Jr., Barry Manilow or John Denver. I'll usually find a song that sticks with me and I'll keep it in my head all day long. I'll just hum it to myself. And that helps maintain rhythm."

Because golf is loaded with tension and stress, music is a natural elixir. "We know from studies that music changes physical and emotional states by dropping people's stress hormones," says Lee S. Berk, an assistant research professor at Loma Linda University. "We are very susceptible to conditioning. If we take something that is calm, it translates into changes in our system."

When she was in her prime, Canadian amateur great Marlene Streit used to sing "Que Sera Sera" to herself as she walked down the fairway, to maintain a good frame of mind. "On your way to your next shot, you've got to fill your mind with something positive and leave no room for negative thoughts," she said. "When I'm teaching a clinic, I tell girls to whistle or sing between shots, even exhale. But once you get to your shot, you stop and go into your pre-shot routine."

Some players prefer spiritual music; Don Massengale used to sing "How Great Thou Art" after a shot. Richard Zokol actually wore headphones for a while in his rookie PGA season of 1982 when he couldn't relax. "I always played worse under pressure, but the music took me to my own world and it was a blast," he recalls. Zokol has since abandoned the practice, partly because it became a distraction to his game and he worried about what people thought, but he is considered a pioneer in the field. His nickname, Disco Dick, sticks to this day.

"I try to make the tension and pressure work for me. I want the adrenaline to be flowing. I think sometimes we try so hard to be cool, calm and collected that we forget what we are doing. There's nothing wrong with being charged up if it's controlled."

— Hale Irwin, three-time U.S. Open champion

CHAPTER 21

CHANGING CHEMISTRY:
Getting Up

W e spend so much time containing our feelings and keeping our arousal levels down — and rightfully so most of the time — we may neglect the excitement and passion of the game. "Sometimes you have to get fired up," says Corey Pavin, who manufactured anger to give himself extra power and focus for two wins in 1995, one with a long wood shot at the 18th hole in the U.S. Open, and again to birdie and win a match at the Ryder Cup.

Most pro golfers keep a lid on their feelings, but not everyone. Tiger Woods saves his fist-pumping and pointing into the hole for big shots, while Dottie Pepper talks to her ball on its way to the hole: "C'mon, baby! C'mon, baby!" When Colin Montgomerie sank a 10-foot putt in the 1999 Ryder Cup, he pumped — or was that punched? — his fist at the sometimes antagonistic American crowd.

Even in friendly matches, amateurs can increase their enjoyment by showing emotion, and having it rub off on their partners. Is there anything more inspiring than a laugh or a little dance on the green?

Without emotions, we are robots. Without emotions at all, there is no feeling or pleasure. Without them, we would not have the desire to play golf. Champions know that pressure and controlled fear can be a source of needed emotions and the hormones they offer as an additive to skills. As he tried to make a comeback in 2000 from an extended slump, six-time majors winner Nick Faldo was pleased with his technical progress, but he couldn't find the extra boost he needed to win a tournament. That boost, he said, was the added adrenaline he would feel when he saw his name on the leader board again. "I'm just outside the real pressure," Faldo said while contending during a stretch of the 2000 European Tour. "It would be nice to be on the leader board, just one or two shots back, and you have to play with that pressure. I haven't quite got into that yet. But there have been enough pressure shots that I played that you can feed off and start to believe if I can put myself in that situation, I can handle it now."

We haven't examined closely enough the science of turning fear from a foe into an ally. Rather than always shutting down the emergency fear system, perhaps we should look at putting it to work at certain times. But when? We should consider it:

- When calming techniques have not brought our nervousness under control.
- When we need an extra boost of power or concentration for a special shot or a short portion of a round.

Performing well under pressure is tricky, and amateurs may want to tinker with techniques special to their personality. Although you need to keep in a relaxed mode for much of your round (otherwise you'll burn out), you can pull fear energy out of your bag like a trusty five-iron. International pro star Ernie Els says he gets nervous "all the time ... you've got to turn it around to your benefit. I try to get excited rather than nervous. If you believe in your game, it will work. Trust your muscle memory. It doesn't work all the time, though."

"It's okay to get upset with yourself for a second, then carry on. It can get your mind back on track," said Ian Leggatt after winning the 2000 Dayton Open on the Buy.com Tour.

I have preached that golfers must find an optimal level of arousal, which differs from person to person, for use over the long haul. We've seen how, if your nervousness becomes excessive, you can get it under control by deep breathing or harness its power by channelling it into your skill, but it takes practice and focus. Elite golfers have shown that at times they can produce an emotional "big bang" of arousal and still be effective. When you do that, though, you had better be able to control the "big bang,"

SOME BIG BANG METHODS

Some ways to get up for a big shot, parts of a round or an entire round:

- thoughts that induce controlled excitement or anger
- reacting to what you consider a threat
- pre-round music or music in your head
- thinking of loved ones
- quick-breathing techniques
- vigorous exercise
- feeding off others' competitiveness
- setting higher goals
- showing a little emotion
- friendly betting

---

or the sudden burst of energy will explode in your swing.

Long before the age of golf psychologists and biochemists, Sam Snead knew the value and results of controlled anger. "You have to learn about yourself; what works for you and what doesn't," Snead said. To become an elite competitive golfer, he said, "I think you need to be very competitive, very driven, but you need to keep an even keel on the course. For me, the right intensity was cool mad. I found a way to stay intense, but just a little bit above the action, on that even keel. It helped me to focus on the next shot instead of spending all my energy trying to calm myself down."

Getting Up with Anger

We can't always dismiss anger as the enemy of golf, because brief periods of controlled anger have shown results. LPGA veteran Dottie Pepper gets nervous when she sees rivals Karrie Webb and Juli Inkster angry. "Don't get Karrie or Juli mad," Pepper says. "I fear them when they're mad. They can come from behind on you." Another LPGA player, Scotland's diminutive Catriona Matthew, used some anger to fortify her determination. Shortly after being (surprisingly) left off the European Solheim Cup team, an unhappy Matthew captured her first tour event, the 2001 Cup Noodles Hawaiian Ladies Open.

Anger may not seem like a positive emotion, but a type of controlled anger can mobilize fear, according to Redford Williams, a professor of psychiatry and psychology at Duke University. Anger gets fear moving forward, he said, by introducing noradrenaline and dopamine into the emergency reaction, "and these are hormones which tend to keep going in the direction you send them. If you begin to think in a confident, aggressive way, they will help you to continue in that mind-set and that physiology."

By becoming angry, you write a prescription for noradrenaline, dopamine and some testosterone. But you must be careful once the fear is transformed into anger, because the latter can take control of you, says Los Angeles psychiatrist Mark Goulston. "The key is to turn anger into focus and determination."

You don't even have to be angry. You can fake it. Sports psychologist James Loehr has proven with research that actors who feign emotions can actually bring the emotions on. If you are stuck in the emotion of fear, perhaps worried that you will lose to a competitor, you can alter your chemistry and mind-set by becoming angry at a colleague or competitor (not to his face but in your head) for taking away some of your business. If you can't find somebody or something to briefly get mad about, try getting angry with yourself. "This is the last time I'm letting myself down!" That sort of thing. You can't let this attitude last for long, because you will succeed in changing your mood from tense and afraid to angry and aggressive for the rest of the day (watch out, it can be seductive). Anger is best used as a short bridge away from fear. After a few seconds, you may be free of your fear long enough to be in a more constructive mood for your shot.

Retief Goosen became briefly infamous for missing a two-foot putt on the 72nd hole of the 2001 U.S. Open, but how many people realize that on the next shot, he got angry with himself long enough to slam a three-footer into the back of the cup to force a playoff, which he won?

Tread softly with anger, though. Biochemists say that if anger or high emotion is kept for a long time, it can be destructive. Long-bombing Grace Park has tried to rid herself of anger in her early years on the LPGA Tour. "It's been a slow process because I got really frustrated and angry on the golf course," she said. "I had to tell myself to stop getting mad, and I'm enjoying myself more now."

Toying with such feelings in golf can be like juggling with dynamite, but it seems to work occasionally when anger is controlled (see the following chapter for more). When she was younger, LPGA hall-of-famer Beth Daniel would get upset after a missed shot and slam her iron into the fairway, but that was fine with her caddy, Greg Sheridan. "I encourage her to misbehave a bit, because it seems to snap her out of whatever she's doing," he said. "It looks bad, but it's part of her personality. If it gets her going, I'm happy."

If anger is an issue in your game, especially in competition, you might want to redirect it. When he was a senior at Oklahoma State, Jeff Lee sometimes threw tantrums after a missed putt and he went on a long losing streak. Then he met sports psychologist Don Greene, who got him to channel the anger by squeezing a golf ball tightly in his hand between putts. "I told him to squeeze it as hard as he could with his left hand, then his right hand, shaking out each hand as he finished," Greene recalls. "Then he was to focus the rest of his energy on making the putt. If he was still pissed off after walking off the green, he was to try to pulverize the ball all over again." Soon, Lee found his anger working for him and later in his senior year he won his first college tournament by beating future PGA star Phil Mickelson in a playoff.

Team golf is rare, but it offers a chance for pep talks, such as captain JoAnne Carner gave to her American team before it won the Solheim Cup in 1994. She recalled when the team arrived and was nervous about the opponents. "Some of the players were talking about how nervous they were. I squelched that right away. I want no negativity. I wanted everything and everybody up. I told them if they were nervous, I would get them some Vaseline for their teeth to quiet the chattering noise."

David Duval recalls what he told his American teammates, who were trailing the Europeans in the 1999 Ryder Cup. "I told them to go out and kill." They did on the closing day, capped by Justin Leonard's incredible 40-foot putt, which touched off a wild celebration.

MUSIC AS AN UPPER

We have already discussed ways that music can help a golfer come down from arousal, but it can work the other way, too. On his way to winning the Ontario Amateur Golf Championship in 1998, Michael Hospodar, a member of the Old Dominion golf team, used the rock tune "Moneytalks" by AC/DC to motivate himself when he hit a bad shot. "When I stumble, I take a deep breath and replay that song in my head, to get aggressive, to get my blood flowing," he said. In 1999, Golf Association of Ontario tournament director Brent McLaughlin shot 69, nine strokes better than his six handicap, by replaying the pop song "Steal My Sunshine" (by the group Len) in his head. "It really helped me when I was nervous with my long-iron approaches to the green on the par-fives," he said. Generally, though, music is used most often as a relaxant, a comforter or a pacer for rhythm.

Thinking of You

*"When the dog bites, when the bee stings, when I'm feeling sad,
I simply remember my favourite things, then I don't feel so bad."*
— from "My Favourite Things," by Rodgers and Hammerstein

Oscar Hammerstein may not have been a low handicapper, but the lyrics of this old tune prove he knew about motivation and human nature. A growing number of elite golfers are learning that thinking of their favourite things helps get them over moments of tension, frustration and pressure.

"If I find myself getting really nervous, I'll turn it off and think about my son or something at home or something I need to do or I haven't done or somebody I was supposed to call and didn't," says LPGA veteran Dale Eggeling.

With this technique, golfers bring a sort of team aspect to a solitary sport. When Korea's Choi Gwang-soo won the 2000 Hyundai Motors Masters on the PGA Davidoff European Tour, he dedicated it to his late father. "I was thinking a lot about my father during my round. I was determined not to lose the title this time."

Scott Hoch won two tournaments, partly for others, at age 45 in 2001. After he triumphed in the Advil Western Open, Hoch said, "I wanted to win this for my old teacher, Richard Tiddy. He's in ill health and he was in the back of my mind. I felt he was helping me get through the pressure of the [final] day." At the Greater Greensboro Classic, Hoch felt inspiration from his old friend, the late Payne Stewart. "I just told him [in thought] to try to help us get through [the final round]. I really felt he was out there with me," said a teary Hoch, who used Stewart's former caddy, Mike Hicks. "When I started feeling a little down, thinking about Payne just turned me around. I just felt kind of a calmness."

Hal Sutton had a similar experience while winning the 2000 Players Championship over a red-hot Tiger Woods. "I did a little talking to old Payne. I said, 'Man, I know you know how to do this, so give me a little help if you can.' I miss Payne a lot and I thought about him a lot [during the tournament]."

In the 1970 British Open, Jack Nicklaus ended a three-year winless skid in the majors, inspired by his father, Charlie, who had died a few months earlier of cancer. Jack felt guilty that he had not adequately fulfilled the legacy his father expected of him. "They've all been for Dad in a way, but never quite like this one," Jack said after tossing his putter high into the air in a rare display of emotion.

Golfers, sometimes without knowing it, can plug into an amazing source of strength in the mind-body, which remains a mystery to scientists yet is gaining credibility because of the many examples becoming public through the media. Thinking of those close to us not only comforts and inspires, it may be nature's programmed way of getting us through a tough time. Check the sports pages and you'll see reports in all sports of athletes whose thinking of loved ones has motivated them through a tough time or stabilized them and offered comfort.

Exercise physiologist Jack Raglin of Indiana University believes this phenomenon is related to the fight-or-flight system, which provides extra power and concentration when we are threatened. "And it places the golf game in context. It tells you what you are doing on a hole isn't as important as the big picture in your life." He suggests that when we are nervous over a shot, we step back and think about things that make us feel warm, then reset over the ball. And we must focus these feelings into our game; otherwise they will be too unwieldy.

Michael Persinger, a neuroscientist at Laurentian University in Sudbury, Ontario, believes that when it comes to these issues, nature knows best — that a human is best motivated under stress when he or she thinks of a loved one. In its most dramatic form, it is probably linked to the phenomenon of what is referred to as a life flashback. "When someone is in a threatening situation, they say their life passed before their eyes," Dr. Persinger said, adding that nature knows such a thought could send a person into the fight-or-flight mode or at least a high level of arousal and sharpened concentration. "It sets off all kinds of chemical and electrical changes in the brain; certainly there is a survival value to this," said Dr. Persinger, who has studied a related phenomenon in which people believe they see ghosts just after a relative dies.

Some golfers, such as Lee Trevino, have pictures of their children with them as they play. Underdog Steve Jones forged briefly into the lead in the 2000 Masters with an autograph of Byron Nelson on his visor. And Rob Cowan won the 2002 Ontario amateur match play championship while using the driver of his father Gary, a legendary amateur. Other golfers keep friends or relatives close to them as caddies, such as Gary Nicklaus, who often had his father Jack as his bag-toter before he made the PGA in 2000.

But perhaps the most personal case of the thinking-of-you technique came in the 1993 Greater Cincinnati amateur championship which Monica Hannah won while nine months pregnant. She thought of it as a twosome.

GOLFERS MOTIVATED BY OTHERS

- In the 1999 State Farm Senior PGA Classic, Christy O'Connor kept his thoughts close to his son Daren (who had died in a car crash). "I won for my son. I know he helped me, looking down from heaven."

- Just prior to the final round of the 1999 U.S. Open, Payne Stewart wept while watching a TV clip about him and his father, then he went out and won with a memorable round. "I probably got a lot of strength from my father," he said.

- The U.S. Women's Open was an LPGA major that eluded Juli Inkster until 1999 when, with her children at her side, she scored an emotional victory.

- In the GTE Byron Nelson Classic of 2000, Davis Love III had "45" inscribed on his cap to commemorate racecar driver Adam Petty's car number after Petty died in a crash just before the tournament.

- Karrie Webb captured the 2001 McDonald's LPGA Championship in honour of her dying grandfather in Australia.

- Richard Zokol snapped a nine-year winless streak by taking the 2001 Samsung Canadian PGA Championship on the Buy.com Tour, partly for his fan Hal Bennett, who was dying of a brain tumour. "He once told me he wouldn't be afraid of dying if I wasn't afraid of winning," Zokol said.

- Greg Reynolds, thinking of his late mother as "an angel on my shoulder," won the 2002 United States Golf Association senior amateur title.

CHAPTER 22

FOCUSING NERVOUSNESS
INTO YOUR SHOT

U nder special circumstances, and for brief periods of time, heightened arousal can actually help your concentration. The crucial trick is to pour all of your energy, especially your nervousness and *fear energy*, into what you are doing and the hell with the consequences — and you might be surprised to learn that you can pull it off. During the primitive days of our evolution, embracing our fear was nature's way of dealing with a difficult physical situation, but nowadays we need to train our fear to work for us rather than against us. It can be like a beast we are trying to domesticate for our use.

As I have already emphasized, the first step in this training is to recognize nervousness as fear. We need to become more aware of our nervousness and its effects on our game. Once we do that, tight focus is the best antidote for fear, according to sports author Dan Millman. "Anyone who has faced a moment of truth, who has felt the fear and leaped from the airplane, walked onto the stage and sat down to the piano or begun speaking to an audience, or otherwise walked to the raw edge and leaped, knows something that more timid souls do not — that once you are fully engaged, immersed in the activity, the fear either vanishes or fades, because your attention is no longer focused on what might happen, you are absorbed by what is happening. Fear may remain, but you don't notice it." Millman added that under pressure, your fears may be in the background, in your subconscious, and they will help you focus even better if you just get into the concentration mode.

In golf, it is essential during times of high nervousness that your thoughts, worries and energies either be calmed or plugged into the process of the swing. It is when we get distracted by the potential outcome that another larger fear is added to the mix, the fear of what might happen: that the tension in our hands may continue, that the shot may go awry and it may hurt our score and, worse, our ego and perhaps even our self-esteem. What will people think of us if we shank? When we become distracted from the process itself, the fear becomes self-destructive and counterproductive. We must worry only about the process and swing away.

If you have your own way of focusing, which has been effective for you in tense situations, stay with it, or perhaps fine-tune it. Good focus keeps many fears under control or at bay, including hazards, noises and opponents, and that allows your energies, including fear energy, to be channelled into your shot. Focus is about disciplining yourself to keep attention on what is important, but it may not come naturally to you.

Cues may be needed to snap back to attention. Remember our discussion of focus from Chapter 15: a cue can be a word you say to yourself ("reload!") or something you force yourself to look at (a sticker on your bag) or a tune you whistle to yourself. And remember to stay in the present; worrying about past mistakes or future consequences can set off your emergency fear system. Seizing the moment lasts a few seconds, long enough for you to focus properly on the shot. The pre-shot routine and visualization will help you.

I have developed a method of focusing during excessive nervousness in which a golfer goes from a fear mode into a less emotional or aroused state. Transforming fear into a more dispassionate state is taking the strong feelings and energies of the emergency fear system and inserting them directly into your shot. The dispassion stage is reached when you allow the nervous passion to be transferred into the process of your shotmaking, then wash your hands of it on a conscious level. Think of it this way: pretend your golf club is a lightning rod for energy, or perhaps a gas pump nozzle you insert into your tank, then allow the high-octane stuff to flow through.

When the high-octane passion becomes a dispassionate skill, such as executing a three-wood from the fairway, you are no longer distracted or self-conscious about the nervous feelings. You have trained the emergency fear system and permitted it to adapt into something productive. Thus the emotions become dispassionate and are channelled into the task. Then the process goes on automatic pilot and becomes an unconscious surrender to one's skills. Occasionally you can reach peak performance with this method and enter what psychologist Robert Nideffer calls getting into the zone. But he recommends that people practise their skill under pressure, to reach the unconscious surrender more often (it doesn't happen all the time, even with scratch golfers). "It is through constant practice that you develop techniques to the point that they can be performed automatically, under highly stressful or competitive conditions," he said. "It is practising until your actions can occur without any conscious thought that leads to your ability to enter the zone and perform to your full potential."

Keep in mind that high arousal is the result of your fear reaction to a pressure situation. Your emergency fear system is working, and it is there to help you, but the energy must be channelled properly or it will turn against you in the form of tension or anxiety as overloads of adrenaline and cortisol get confused about what they should be doing. You must give them purpose or your performance will suffer and you may even choke. If you can capture this two-stage formula — fear to dispassionate response — stick with it. Keep things as simple as possible. It may not work right away, or it may not work all the time. You may need to try it under various circumstances. With practice, the method will improve. Don't give up on it after one or two tries, and don't expect to plug your arousal into a task for which you are not adequately trained, such as a 15-handicapper going for the flag with a two-wood out of the rough.

Many readers of my 30-week psychology column on the internet reported success with this formula in their golf game and in their business dealings off the course. But others struggled with consistently getting into the focus stage. If that is a problem, I recommend allowing a few seconds to bridge between the fear and the dispassion. It should be a very brief time-out, and you can refer to this as a neutral stage. High arousal is a type of overdrive of your emergency fear system and not all of us can gear this directly into our golf game, so we need a brief shift into neutral as a go-between. To shift into the neutral time-out, you may want to use a mantra word or phrase by thinking to yourself or saying aloud something like "neutral" or "let go." For example, when you are trying to carry a five-iron over water and you are jittery over the ball, take an exaggerated breath and tell yourself, "out of the way!"

When you relax and let go, you get out of your own way. And getting in your own way (or trying too hard) is often what causes too much pressure in the first place. This technique can also return you to a more manageable level of arousal, which moods expert Robert Thayer calls calm energy (the mood or emotional state in which we are alert but in control). In the end, when you can return yourself to tight focus, the nervous distraction will dissipate.

If you continue to have problems with focus, you should practise the technique on the range, stimulating arousal by thinking of important shots and pressure scenarios.

A quick review of this two-stage formula:

1. **Feel the fear.** Recognize your arousal as fear energy. There are no feelings of nervousness without fear, but it is there to help you in a tough spot. Feel glad and confident when you feel it. It will make you stronger physically and sharper mentally.

2. **Change the fear to dispassionate focus or skills.** Redirecting fear energy into your game removes distractions and focuses the energy on the task at hand, on the process and not the potential results. You may want to use a cue word or phrase for a brief period of neutral transition. If the dispassionate focus does not kick in after one or two seconds, hold on a short time longer while focusing on your shot.

The Alliance of Golf Emotions

There is another way to redirect fear and nervousness for positive effect. Rather than the two-stage method of fear-to-dispassion, it is a little more complicated. I call it the alliance of emotions, and here is its technique: fear-to-passion-to-dispassionate response. It involves adding another emotion to prevent fear from locking you into a freeze mode. Such feelings as excitement, levity, love and even anger, motivate us and get us moving forward, which is exactly what fear must do if it is to become productive; otherwise we can choke. So we get fear moving, flowing with excitement or joy, as a river, an alliance. This creates not only a river in the mind-body but in the whole routine of the golf shot, and it provides us with more confidence. (At the outset, anger may not seem like a positive emotion and yet a type of controlled anger can provide a proactive purpose by mobilizing fear. It, too, can spark a unity, a flow of emotion.)

First of all, you must become aware that your nervousness has gone beyond the point where it can be corrected through calming techniques or channelling through focus. Then you must embrace this fear very briefly with another passionate emotion, such as excitement or anger. The third stage is to pour the passion into the process of our golf swing, a very dispassionate ending. Here are the three steps in review:

1. **Feel the fear.** Recognize the arousal as fear. There are no feelings of nervousness without fear, but it is there to help you in a tough spot.
2. **Change it to passion.** This alters the brain chemistry to more aggressive, mobilizing hormones.
3. **Change passion to dispassion.** Suddenly turning off your thinking sends the hormones into muscle memory, and that can help your performance in terms of giving you longer distance, sharpened concentration and fewer distractions.

To get from Stages 1 to 2, it's helpful to use cue words. Changing the emotion of fear to that of passion brings action to the process. Passion is an individual thing and can be viewed as challenge or excitement or anger. The shift in thinking drastically alters the chemical makeup of the mind-body and removes much of the overflow of adrenaline, which is primarily a defensive hormone that can make us seize up. Fear immobilizes a person but action tends to replace adrenaline with noradrenaline and dopamine, both aggressive hormones.

The final stage involves putting the passion into the skill of the task, whether it is the first tee shot of the day in front of a crowd or making an approach to a small green or facing a crucial five-foot putt. Thus the emotions become dispassionate and are channelled into the shot. Then the process goes on automatic pilot and becomes an unconscious surrender to one's skill, without worrying about the consequences ... although the skill is heightened with the arousal hormones.

The formula must be carried out swiftly and with a degree of flow: fear-to-passion-to-dispassion. I recommend the technique be started just before the pre-shot routine and come to an end as you become absorbed in the pre-shot routine. Golfers and other people in pressure situations sometimes discover this formula through trial and mostly error, and yet its existence is not widely known, or not articulated clearly. If we could understand it better in our society of intense competition, we would not allow fear to be as debilitating as it is. In fact, like the most successful golfers, we might embrace it as an ally.

A final note: rather than having me instruct you *exactly* on how to change your chemistry on the golf course, use your own imagination, incorporating some of the above ideas.

Here is a breakdown of some emotions you might want to trigger to ally with your fear. While this is an inexact science, studies have shown such an alliance can work. You may want to experiment with each of them at various times and decide which is best for you in a certain situation.

THE PASSIONATE EMOTIONS: EXCITEMENT

- **Description**: This is a broad emotion, but can be effective because it is passionate in a positive sense and can get fear energy mobilized. It may be too unwieldy for some people, yet it's a good starting point from which you can narrow your focus through trial and practice.
- **Hormones it can trigger**: dopamine, noradrenaline, some adrenaline.
- **Mind-set**: I am going to enjoy this round! I am going to be satisfied or rewarded, either by my score or by the progress I make or by the enjoyment I will get through the experience or camaradarie. I will not be beaten by fear. Success is a split-second away!
- **Situations to think about**: There will be birdie chances on those par threes you usually do well on. You can't wait to get to that beautiful No. 3 hole surrounded by water. Soon you will be hearing Johnny's giggle over his misfortune in a sand trap.
- **Real-life example**: Amateur Anthony Roma of West Palm Beach was worried about his upcoming match-play event against an opponent he had lost to by three and four holes in the past. He changed his thinking and suddenly looked forward to the chance to improve his performance. He maintained his sense of excitement throughout the match and lost by just one hole.

THE PASSIONATE EMOTIONS: ANGER

- **Description**: It can be an unwieldy, explosive feeling, but it's a surefire way to get fear mobilized. If you are going to use anger as an embracing emotion, you must make sure you are familiar with its feelings, its allure of power and control, and its potential spillovers.

- **Hormones it can trigger**: noradrenaline, dopamine, testosterone (especially through thoughts of dominance), cortisol and some adrenaline.

- **Mind-set**: Dammit, I will not give in. I'll show them. And I will certainly not let myself down and ruin all the practising I've done. I refuse to let my colleagues or myself down. I can't let this chance for extra power and control get away.

- **Situations to think about**: The ways you've let yourself down in the past with lack of discipline or patience. A competitor taking your rewards away. A time you felt you were wronged over a ruling.

- **Real-life example**: At times during the 2001 Buick Classic, Sergio Garcia was able to bear down and in a way seek revenge by thinking about criticism he had received: his swing supposedly needed changing and his father, Victor, was his swing coach. After Sergio went on to win, he declared, "[The critics] are going to have to eat all those words that they said."

THE PASSIONATE EMOTIONS: LOVE

- **Description**: This emotion is a strong feeling you forge for loved ones, acquaintances, co-workers or a team or your club. You become aroused to win the day for them whether in a competitive or social sense.
- **Hormones it can trigger**: DHEA, serotonin, oxytocin.
- **Mind-set**: You imagine a clear picture of a loved one. Don't worry, I'm there for you! I'll try my best not to let you down.
- **Situations to think about**: Your spouse, your children, the members of your foursome.
- **Real-life example**: Vijay Singh used to be known as the best player never to have won a PGA major, but he learned to trust himself by putting a sign made by his young son on his golf bag: Papa, Trust Your Swing. Whenever he felt afraid in a pressure situation, Singh looked at his son's words. He went on to win two majors.

THE PASSIONATE EMOTIONS: LEVITY

- **Description**: This is a tricky one because humour is usually thought of as something to defuse fear, rather than as a passionate ally. But it can be done. This emotion not only produces relaxation, but power and control in a pressing situation, especially if we think of something really funny, not just amusing. If there was no natural connection with fear, endorphins would not be released. You laugh because fear left alone without an embracing emotion is painful. And the mind-body responds with painkilling endorphins.

- **Hormones it can trigger**: endorphins, serotonin, even dopamine and noradrenaline in certain instances.

- **Mind-set**: Hah! I will survive. No situation is above laughter, whether it is a buried lie or a sudden glitch in my swing. Trouble, I laugh in your face because I know I have fear hormones as my ally.

- **Situations to think about**: If my opponent is so threatening, why does the silly bugger have mustard stains on his expensive shirt?

- **Real life example**: High handicapper Sue Green of Long Island, N.Y., was getting too serious about her technical game falling apart. But when she saw her intense, ugly reflection in a pond while searching for her ball, she burst out laughing. For the rest of the round, she referred to herself as the Wicked Witch of the Front Nine and suddenly she didn't try as hard and her score improved, not to mention her enjoyment.

THE PASSIONATE EMOTIONS: CONFIDENCE

- **Description**: To many, this is a fuzzy emotion or a state of mind. But if we consider it to be an emotion, it may be more effective in channeling our hormones and other resources into a task.
- **Hormones it triggers**: adrenaline, noradrenaline, dopamine, some endorphins and serotonin.
- **Mind-set**: I have competent resources and most of the time they will bring me success.
- **Situations to think about**: Past successes.
- **Real-life example**: On the 72nd hole of the 2000 Canadian Open, Tiger Woods' lead was threatened when his tee shot went into a fairway bunker, 225 yards from a green protected by a lake. Woods was nervous and considered laying up his second shot, but told himself, "I'm Tiger Woods!" His six-iron incredibly sailed over the water to a position where he two-putted for the victory.

"I was hitting the ball so badly, but I kept fighting. I just fought and fought and fought."

— Ben Dickerson of Hilliard, Florida, after winning a match in the 2000 U.S. Amateur Public Links Championship

CHAPTER 23

THE CHARACTER TEST:
Becoming a Grinder

For much of the 2001 PGA Tour, something about Tiger Woods' game was off. His booming tee shots were hooking or fading more than usual; he was not bolting out of the gate with 65s to start tournaments and the magic in his putter had lost some of its sparkle. And yet, partly through determination and guts, Woods managed to win five tournaments, including the Masters, $5.7 million (U.S.) and Player of the Year.

Woods showed the golf world that he was human (some critics started calling him by his real name, Eldrick) and that his technical game was indeed mortal, but he also showed he could be an above-average *grinder*, a golfer who overcomes problems through sheer determination. "In many tournaments, I was proud of the way I fought through problems and situations," he said.

Woods learned grinding from Jack Nicklaus. "He taught me that you don't have to be on top of your game to win. In one of our conversations [during the 2000 PGA Championship]," Woods said, "he told me, 'I very seldom won with my A game. I won with my

B game and my C game, and I managed. You have the same thing.'"
We may think of Woods and Nicklaus as overpowering talents, but
they are also consummate grinders, who win not only with their
long balls, but also with long patience, discipline and not giving in
to negative emotions. "My short game was a weakness, but that
was because I felt I didn't need it," Nicklaus said. "I won without
it. I think if I had needed it, I would have worked on it."

The best male amateur of all time, Bobby Jones, was a grinder
who won the 1930 British amateur championship and the British
Open with his bounce-back mentality. He said, "By the hardest
possible kind of labour, I managed to win these two tournaments
when my game was never once anywhere near peak efficiency."

If your friends call you a grinder, accept it as the ultimate
compliment. Grinders are golfers who never give up in the
course of a round, despite bad shots, bad breaks and the pressure
to score well. Grinders probably don't choke as much as other
players because they know they can fight through. It is probably
better to be born a grinder than to be born with raw talent.

Besides being good for your game, becoming a grinder can
show your character and help you gain the respect of your peers.
"Competitive golf can be like life: a test. It can reflect how you live
your life and how patient you can be," says LPGA player Cristie Kerr.
"It's about how you handle the good breaks and the bad breaks."

The main character test is taking responsibility, Nicklaus says.
"Accept one cold fact — that every single shot you hit, good or
bad, is the product of only one person: you. Don't blame outside
factors like the course or the weather or your clubs. Too many
players do that and they don't improve. They're not realistic
with themselves." Remember that when you hear players
constantly complaining that they could have played well, "but

> **CHARACTER QUIZ**
>
> Are you a grinder? How would you rate yourself in the following important categories of golf?
>
> - patience
> - discipline
> - determination
> - inspiration
> - honesty
> - focus (in shotmaking and in putting things in perspective)
> - self-awareness
>
> You may be stronger in some areas than others. Just as in your technical golf game, shore up your weaknesses.

the putts just weren't dropping," it sounds as though playing well only involves woods and irons and that putting is left to chance, out of the control of the golfer.

In their book, *Shrink Your Handicap*, Phil Lee and Jeff Warne refer to this attitude as "the blame game," in which golfers assign blame for a bad shot to others. "The greenskeeper for poor lies on the tee, the partners who talked during our backswing, even our parents who didn't have good genes or didn't teach us properly. This is an immature response. Mortification and embarrassment and shame and humiliation are the true underlying emotions of the (psychologically) average golfer after hitting a bad shot in public. These are also the responses of children scolded or ridiculed for things they know they shouldn't have done. We must exorcize the blame game; we need to uninstall it."

However, PGA veteran Dave Stockton likes it when many excuses are available to his opponents. He says, "Give me the wind, bad weather, bumpy greens and slow play — it all gives me an advantage because I know I'm mentally prepared to handle it while a lot of other players aren't." That's because Stockton considers himself a grinder.

In recent years, sports psychology has added greatly to understanding the mental side of golf, but some sports psychologists and golf teachers may be contributing to the blame game. Some suggest to players that a poor round must have been the fault of their clubs, or the course just wasn't suited for their game.

Character *can* improve your score and can keep you going when there's a bug in your swing or when your score is getting embarrassing. It can be as tangible as anything in your bag, so hold your character aloft, like a nine-iron (without rubbing it in your opponent's face).

"You've done a lot of living and have all sorts of experiences stored in your memory that can be used to generate appropriate states of mind for playing golf," says Marlin M. Mackenzie, a counsellor to amateur and professional golfers. "These resource states include optimism, eagerness, determination, calmness, inventiveness, hopefulness, acceptance, patience, friendliness, sensitivity to nature and a lot more."

If we want to impress others, why not do it with a gritty comeback after a poor front nine or showing determination out of hazards? The greens are a good proving ground, to reveal we are not afraid to go boldly after a birdie or be confident with a par-saving putt. Believe it or not, your opponents may remember your grace under adversity long after the ink fades on your scorecard. Strong character (as well as emotional team bonding) is what has kept Europe in contention with the sometimes more talented American team in Ryder Cup action over the years.

In the moment of truth, with a match on the line, you may find that inner strength gives you an edge in making a crucial shot or recovering from trouble. Grinders don't panic if they happen to choke on a shot. Everybody gets nervous and rattled under pressure from time to time. "Choking is not synonymous with having a flawed character," says Bob Rotella. "Some nasty, miserable people have triumphed under pressure. And some of the finest, most admirable human beings have choked in tight situations." And yet such situations eventually help people learn to deal with pressure and internal fears, he added.

Cheating: The Fastest Cart

A discussion on the subject of character usually gets around to honesty. Do you cheat? "He who has the fastest golf cart never has a bad lie," joked baseball great Mickey Mantle, who played a lot of golf.

"Because golf performance so readily becomes tied to feelings of overall self-worth, the game brings out the fraud in people more than most other games," writes psychologist Alan Shapiro in *Golf's Mental Hazards*. "The golfer's score impacts on handicap, and handicap becomes a defining quality of identity. As a result, there is a potentially face-saving, status-building motive to cheat."

We all probably take a mulligan from time to time, but we can still retain our dignity if we don't cheat to a large degree and if we try to put a stop to it, says Shapiro. "Because golf imitates life, consider the fraud that comprises the rest of your life," he said. "Do you cheat at cards, on your income tax, on your spouse? Do you lie a lot or a little, exaggerating details to make yourself appear wealthier, smarter or more athletic? If you do, welcome to the club. None of us are so godly as to be entirely self-assured and comfortable with who we are."

When a player informs an unaware tournament official that he or she has double-hit or accidentally moved the ball with a practice swing, we admire the honesty in the face of the penalty. If that happens to us, let's report it with pride. Honesty can also be important to self-improvement. If we choose to blindly defend ourselves and our score and don't face the truth about our game, chances are we will likely keep repeating the same swings that got us into the cheating position in the first place.

Losing with grace is another hall of fame trait. In 1961, Arnold Palmer won a great friend in his rival Gary Player. When defending champion Palmer lost by one stroke to Player in the Masters, he didn't sulk but rather slipped the green jacket on the winner with a glowing speech of praise that remained fresh in Player's memory decades later.

Caring for the game of others in your foursome may also reap you rewards and respect. Without these things, isn't golf too much of a game of sticks and holes and self-absorption? Perhaps those of us who follow the professional golf tours should start choosing our golfing heroes by the character they show and the principles they stand for, rather than their trophies, which just gather dust in a glass case.

Good Lies? How Golfers Deceive Themselves

While most pro golfers are probably honest, some try to make the game less neurotic by fibbing to the media and perhaps even to themselves.

Without the honesty and insights of many professional golfers into the often queasy subject of why golfers choke, this book would not have been possible. But sometimes we can't exactly believe some of the world's top golfers when they deny having let their emotions get the better of them, when there is evidence to suggest that they have.

When Tiger Woods seemed to fib to the world's media after making two crucial bogeys at the 2002 PGA Championship, he joined the company of his idol Jack Nicklaus by ignoring the facts, apparently to protect his competitive psyche. After his round, Woods told the press that an eagle that put Rich Beem ahead for good did not cause him to three-putt on No. 13 at Hazeltine National Golf Club in Minneapolis and then to make an awful tee shot with a four-iron on No. 14, even though his body language and expression seemed to droop with despair and perhaps even fear. When told that a TV broadcaster said he had choked, Woods replied, "Sometimes they have no idea what they're talking about."

If Tiger lied to the media, or to himself, he had some prestigious company : the great Nicklaus, winner of 18 majors, who claims he has never three-putted within five feet on the last hole of an event, although there is taped evidence to show otherwise. According to golf psychologist Bob Rotella, such self-deception is "selective amnesia … Jack was a talented putter. He was able to block from his mind all the missed putts. He kept and replayed the memories of made putts. He was able to retain a firm belief that the next one was going in the hole. He was able to think of himself as a great putter. Because he thought that way, he was able to be a great putter." That is ironic, because Nicklaus and most other pros have steel-trap memories after a round and can usually recall the minutest details of every shot.

Such self-deception is often encouraged by some of today's sports psychologists, who fill golfers' heads with only positive thoughts. Perhaps that's why many golfers blame outside forces rather than admit they made a mistake, or that they choked. The wind blew their putt off line, they say, or their ball landed in a fairway divot or it was the fault of their putter, so they throw it out. Canadian fan favourite Lorie Kane jokes that her LPGA errors are the fault of an evil imaginary twin sister.

Some psychologists say such techniques can be helpful over the short term, reassuring a golfer that he or she is indeed a great player, but denying weaknesses for too long, such as a mediocre short game, can hurt.

For the average duffer, golf instructors and psychologists say it might be more productive to admit failures and flaws (even things we may consider character flaws) to improve or even just to better enjoy the game. It really is quite okay to choke occasionally because, as we've seen, even the best golfers do. But Rotella reminds us that the average golfer cannot really relate to the psyche of Woods or Nicklaus. When a Nicklaus fan told Rotella he was disappointed with Jack's fibbing, the psychologist retorted, "You're a 16 handicap ... you want Jack to think like you?"

Bouncing Back from Lousy Things

"Truly great players do not roll over and die after a disaster."
— John Feinstein, from his book *The Majors*

Surviving danger is one of the hallmarks of a grinder. "I've always considered myself a pretty good scrambler out of trouble," Tiger Woods says. "I grew up in trees, thanks to my dad."

Even when you lose it emotionally, you should try to recover by laughing at yourself. Said the legendary Bobby Jones of tossing a club in frustration, "Sometimes the game of golf is just too difficult to endure with a golf club in your hands."

You may not be a great player as far as physical skills go, but you can always prove your mental toughness. Watch how Woods responds after he has a bad shot or a bad hole. In the 2000 U.S. Open at Pebble Beach, Woods' tee shot sank into the ocean and a little later he had a triple-bogey. Tiger responded to those blips by immediately fighting back with a par, by getting his rhythm back on track, back to record a championship performance.

Woods has learned this wonderful habit through mental toughness. He is always up among the statistical leaders in the *bounce-back* category. About one-third of the time, he has responded to a bogey by scoring under par on the very next hole. Woods and other great players understand that golf is often a game of survival, especially under pressure. Everybody chokes occasionally, but it's how we react to a situation that sets us apart.

Maybe, after a shank or a poor hole, we should give ourselves a *character point* if we don't let it drag us down. The pros are masters at this. "What really matters in golf is resiliency," says Hale Irwin. A chance to show our mettle from the rough, or from a day in which our swing is off, can give us more satisfaction than a birdie, not to mention practice in creativity. If you are becoming a grinder, this is your signature shot. "Golf is like life," says veteran golf teacher Jim Flick. "You must be able to learn from failure."

"Learn to play badly, and enjoy it!" says British golf coach Vivien Saunders. "Anyone can cope with playing well; the art is to learn to cope with playing badly. If you can still survive and enjoy the game after a horrendous day, you suddenly find they aren't so likely to happen. If you panic, then bad turns to worse.

Obviously, to be a champion, you have to have self pride. You want to do your best. You can't be complacent. But fear of bad scores is, in the main, what causes them."

From an emotional standpoint, teaching pros and psychologists offer us many techniques on how to act after disaster strikes, from deep breathing to humour to visualizing the next shot to replacing doubt and bad memories with memories of good shots.

Poor reaction can result in mind-body arousal, according to psychologist Alan Shapiro, who gives workshops to golfers and recommends positive thinking and relaxation after a wayward shot. "Each time you face an anger-provoking situation, your heart starts racing, your stomach begins to churn and your body burns oxygen at a faster rate," he said. "A cleansing breath, a burst of fresh oxygen, released muscular tension, and at least for a brief moment, things will not seem all that unmanageable."

Calvin Kupeyan of the University of Nevada at Las Vegas keeps things in perspective. "I've learned that if I bogey a hole, it's not the end of the world, that golf is just a game," Kupeyan said after winning the 2000 Ontario men's amateur championship.

"If you hit a bad shot, just tell yourself it is great to be alive, relaxing and walking around on a beautiful golf course," says Al Geiberger, who is the co-holder of the PGA record for a low round with 59. "The next shot will be better."

Think of a mistake as a mental divot, one that you will replace before going on to the next shot. And it *is* the next shot. Remember that golf is more of a marathon than a sprint. "If I miss a three-footer, I take a deep breath and tell myself I've taken a million three-footers; most of them go in but once in a while they don't," says two-time LPGA winner Gail Graham. "You have to forget about the bad things which will happen once in a while and stay in the present for the next shot."

LPGA star Sherri Steinhauer pretends her memory is a video machine. If something happens she does not want repeated, she erases the tape in her mind.

EMOTIONS TIP: BOUNCING BACK

Sometimes we can transfer our ability to recover in our personal lives and put it into our golf game. PGA players Paul Azinger, Larry Nelson, Arnold Palmer and Gene Littler all overcame cancer and returned to the tour. Casey Martin rode a cart to hold off a crippling disease, and four-time PGA winner Al Balding won the 2000 Canadian PGA seniors title at age 76, after beating bone cancer, several shoulder surgeries and quadruple-bypass surgery just two years earlier.

At age 15, Retief Goosen was struck by lightning on a golf course. He was knocked unconscious, his clothes burned off and his shoes melted. But two weeks later he was playing golf again. Little wonder that in 2001, Goosen bounced back from a missed two-foot putt on the 72nd hole to capture the U.S. Open by one-putting seven of the first nine holes to win the next day's 18-hole playoff.

When amateur golfer Tom Pansing, a Phoenix architect, gets negative thoughts "trying to benumb me" from bad shooting, he does not allow them to dominate. Rather, he goes into an "action-focused state" and makes sure he tries to enjoy his golf outing.

Like Tiger Woods, one of Karrie Webb's key weapons is her ability to bounce back. Prior to the final round of the 2000 U.S.

Women's Open, leader Meg Mallon feared this about Webb, her rival. "The most amazing thing to me is that when she does make a mistake, she'll reel off three birdies in a row. That's why she's so difficult to beat." Mallon's words came true hours later as Webb overcame a sloppy front nine to overtake Mallon and win the title. Webb later said she rejected her tendency to choke on a few holes "by thinking of good memories from past tournaments I've won. I use those things as a bonus."

Bad shots, though, make the psychology of golf more complicated. They can lead to changes in strategy for the next shot, and not always in a positive way. Golf psychiatrist Phil Lee cautions golfers not to alter their thinking drastically to make up for a poor shot, especially if their confidence wanes a little. "Our natural urge is to go for a big shot, to get it all back," he said. "You think that, 'Well, now I'm behind after a poor drive, I have to try the miracle shot through the trees to get even.' But after giving up a shot on a hole, it makes no sense to go all out for par. Building confidence merges with grinding it out, which to a large extent means playing within yourself."

And yet, being human, we should allow ourselves the occasional rant after a slice into deep grass. "It's human nature to get negative thoughts and doubts after a poor shot, especially in an important situation," says LPGA veteran Nancy Harvey, who took psychology at Arizona State University. But the true mark of a champion is the ability to recover after this fickle game deals you a blow to the tummy, as it will do a number of times every round — as Arnold Palmer did in the 1961 British Open when he used a six-iron to rescue his ball from a nearly-impossible lie in deep rough to preserve his lead, or as Seve Ballasteros did in the 1983

Ryder Cup when he shined with a four-wood from a fairway bunker on the 18th hole.

Another valuable trait is the ability to bounce back after a frustrating tournament. Jean Van de Velde became the laughingstock of world media when he had a triple-bogey on the final hole of the 1999 British Open, needing just a double-bogey to win. He could easily have folded, but he chuckled at himself after losing the playoff at Carnoustie. "I walked into the press conference and looked into the faces of the journalists," he said. "It was like it was the end of the world. Well, I'm sorry, it wasn't. I had it in my hand and I threw it away. But I'm still comfortable with myself." Although he's not a player of unforgettable skills, Van de Velde recovered in the 2000 season and became a regular on the PGA Tour. And the easygoing Frenchman inspired an internet fan club with the rallying cry, "Allez, Jean!" (Go for it, Jean!)

Some fans remember Bernard Langer as the guy who blew a makeable putt as Europe lost to the U.S. in the 1991 Ryder Cup, but few realize he rebounded the following week to win another tournament. "I looked at it this way. There was only one perfect man in this world — and they crucified Him," Langer said. "All I did was miss a putt." Greg Norman is often called a choker by fans and media, and yet he gained the respect of thousands of golf fans around the world, who showered him with letters and e-mails after he showed courage and dignity despite blowing the 1996 Masters. Nick Price told Norman, "You've earned more respect and more friends by handling yourself the way you did in the adversity that you faced than if you'd won three Masters in a row."

Sometimes, bouncing back after a disappointing 18 holes means admitting your game isn't good enough and needs help.

In the spring of 2000, Mark Keast, editor of the *Canadian* PGA *Golf Magazine*, shot 101 at a course in Burlington, Ontario. "Even the cigar smoke in the jeep on the drive back couldn't wipe away the lingering stench of a bad golf round," Keast wrote. And so, for the first time in his 20 years of six or seven rounds a season, Keast sought out a teaching pro, who helped him gain confidence with a few basic changes in his grip, setup and posture. Subsequently, Keast was able to manage his game better and reduce the pressure that caused frustration and choking.

By using that strategy, along with the other three strategies we have discussed throughout this book — being aware of what makes you nervous, focusing effectively and managing your emotional chemistry — we can make golf less fearful and more fun.

GLOSSARY

This is a quick reference for some of the terms in this book:

adrenaline: a powerful hormone unleashed throughout your body when you feel threatened

alliance of emotions: linking fear with another emotion to help a golfer plug the hormones into the swing

arousal: the feelings and powers released by the emergency fear system

belly putter: an elongated putter anchored against the stomach or sternum, reducing the pressure on the wrists and hands for the putting stroke

big muscles: your upper arms and legs, and torso muscles used for power in the golf swing

choking: when emotions, particularly fear, negatively interfere with a golfer's normal technique, focus or decision making

claw grip: a putting style in which one hand is held conventionally and the fingers of the other hand are placed across the
grip rather than around it

cortisol: a hormone released to help you meet threats over the
long haul; too much worry can cause anxiety, releasing
enough cortisol to make you ill

dopamine: a hormone that tends to make you aggressive and
gives you emotional momentum

ego defence: evoking your fear defence system to protect your
ego or pride

emotional chemistry: the flow of hormones in your system,
activated by emotions

emotional drive: the determination you have to succeed over
the long haul

endorphin: a hormone that acts as a painkiller and is also
released when you laugh, making you feel good

emergency fear system: a complex system that some people
generally refer to as the sympathetic nervous system; it
reacts whenever you feel a threat, providing you with extra
strength and speed and enhanced concentration

fear defence system: a powerful resource for reacting to
threats; it has two branches, the emergency fear system and
the worry system

fear energy: the energy produced by hormones released
through the emergency fear system

flow: an "in-the-zone" experience in which everything seems
effortless

fight or flight: the ultimate response of the emergency fear
system, designed to help you overcome a serious threat

grinder: a golfer who fights through problems or days when he or she is not playing well in a technical sense

hyper flow: a heightened sense of awareness in which the golfer can sometimes perform at a higher level

pressure: the demands you feel from outside forces, other people or your internal expectations

serotonin: a hormone linked with inner peace, creates relaxation and happiness

small muscles: your wrists and fingers, which can be sensitive to bouts of nervousness

visualization: a technique used by golfers to mentally picture how their swing will go and the path their ball will take, always imagining a successful conclusion

worry system: part of the fear defence system that deals with long-term threats and challenges

yips: nervous bouts experienced by golfers, usually associated with putting woes

zone: a mental and sometimes physical state in which the golfer can seemingly do no wrong

SUGGESTED READING

Alder, Harry and Karl Morris, *Masterstroke*, Piatkus Publishers, 1996

Beck, Chip and Wayne Glad, *Focused for Golf*, Human Kinetics, 1999

Behrens, Richard, *Golf, The Winner's Way*, Llewellyn, 1999

Clarkson, Michael, *Intelligent Fear*, Key Porter, 2002

Cohn, Patrick J., *The Mental Game of Golf*, Diamond Communications, 1994

Coop, Richard with Bill Fields, *Mind Over Golf*, Macmillan, 1991

Dozier , Rush W., Jr., *Fear Itself*, St. Martin's, 1998

Feinstein, John, *The Majors*, Little, Brown and Company, 1999

Gallwey, W. Timothy, *The Inner Game of Golf*, Random House, 1981

Graham, Deborah and Jon Stabler, *The Eight Traits of Champion Golfers*, Fireside, 1999

Hallowell, Edward M., *Connect*, Pocket Books, 2001

Jackson, Susan A. and Mihaly Csikszentmihalyi, *Flow in Sports*, Human Kinetics, 1999

Loehr, James E., *The New Toughness Training for Sports*, Plume, 1995

MacClure, Terrence, *Golf Ching*, Andrews McMeel Publishing, 1997

MacKenzie, Marlin M., *Golf: The Mind Game,* Dell, 1990

MacRury, Downs, *Golfers on Golf*, Barnes and Noble, 2001

McCord, Gary , *Golf for Dummies*, Hungry Minds Inc., 1999

Nicklaus, Jack, *Jack Nicklaus' Playing Lessons*, Pocket Books, 1976

Nicklaus, Jack with Ken Bowden, *Jack Nicklaus, My Story*, Simon and Schuster, 1997

Nideffer, Robert M., *Psyched to Win*, Human Kinetics, 1992

Palmer, Arnold with James Dodson, *A Golfer's Life*, Ballantine, 1999

Peck, M. Scott, *Golf and the Spirit*, Three Rivers Press, 1999

Pelz, Dave, *Dave Pelz's Putting Bible*, Doubleday, 2000

Post, Sandra and Loral Dean, *Sandra Post and Me*, McClelland and Stewart, 1998

Rosaforte, Tim, *Raising the Bar*, St. Martin's, 2000

Rotella, Bob, *Golf Is Not a Game of Perfect,* Simon and Schuster, 1995

Rotella, Bob, *Putting Out of Your Mind*, Simon and Schuster, 2001

Sampson, Curt, *Hogan*, Broadway, 1996

Shapiro, Alan, *Golf's Mental Hazards,* Fireside, 1996

Shoemaker, Fred with Pete Shoemaker, *Extraordinary Golf*, Perigee Books, 1996

Snead, Sam, *The Game I Love*, Ballantine Books, 1997

St John, Lauren, *Shark: The Biography of Greg Norman*, Rutledge Hill Press, 1998

Thayer, Robert E., *The Origins of Everyday Moods*, Oxford, 1996

Valentine, Linda and Margie Hubbard, *Golf Games Within the Game*, Perigee, 1992

Wilks, Frances, *Intelligent Emotion*, Arrow, 1998

INDEX

INDEX

Clark, Michael, 71
claw grip putting, 217, 218
clubs, 102, 103–4, 175
Cohn, Patrick J., 52–53, 120, 141, 161–62, 175, 177–78, 208
Coleman, Theresa, 42
concentration, 182, 184, 190–91
confidence, 124–33, 220, 273
controlled anger, 89–90, 254
Cook, John, 190
Cookson, David, 23–24
Coop, Dick, 143
Cooper, Alice, 165
cortisol, 36–37, 40, 94, 137
Couples, Fred, 63, 178, 217
Cowan, Gary, 61, 207
Cowan, Rob, 260
Crenshaw, Ben, 75
cross-handed putting, 217
Csikszentmihalyi, Mihaly, 197–98, 199, 201
cues, 203, 263–64
Curtis, John D., 94

D'Alessio, Diana, 131
Daly, John, 171–72, 244, 245
Daniel, Beth, 142, 256
Das, Y.P., 137
Davenport, Paul, 189
Davies, Laura, 87, 155, 171–72
defence mechanisms, 50–51. *See also* subconscious
Delsing, Jay, 88
desensitization, 152–55
DHEA, 36–37
Diaz, Jaime, 27–28
Diaz, Laura, 65, 99
Dickerson, Ben, 274
Didrickson, Babe, 131
Dienstbier, Richard, 144
DiMarco, Chris, 65
distractions, 152–53, 188, 189–91, 201
distress, 42
Dobbs, Frank, 155
Doolan, Wendy, 188
dopamine, 36–37, 91
Douglas, Richard, 239–40

Douillard, John, 200–201
Doyle, Allen, 174
Dunbar, John, 136
Dunlap, Reg, 88
Duval, David, 189, 206, 257
dystonia, 69

Eala, Jovey M., 174
Eggeling, Dale, 247, 258
ego defence, 50–55, 117–18
Ehrich, Brian, 194
elation, 239
Eliot, Robert, 49
Els, Ernie, 190, 253
embarrassment, 24–31, 117–19, 149–52
emergency fear system, 29–30, 34–35
emotional chemistry, 18, 223–73
endorphin, 36–37
enjoyment of golf, 161–68
Epstein-Shepherd, Bee, 211, 214
equipment, 102, 103, 175
eustress, 42
Evans, Chick, Jr., 202
exercise, and flow, 203

failure, fear of, 25–26, 180
Faldo, Nick, 217, 246–47, 252
Falvey, Patrick, 136, 216
Farron, Susan, 136
Fasciana, Guy S., 132
Faxon, Brad, 206
fear, 41–42, 45, 49–50, 68, 93–94;
    managing, 18, 235, 252, 262–68;
    of other's opinions (allodoxaphobia),
    24–31, 117–19. *See also* arousal; stress
fight-or-flight response, 35, 44
fine motor control, 63, 215–16
Finney, Allison, 116
first tee jitters, 211–15
Flick, Jim, 176, 283
flow zone, 84–85, 86–89, 197–201
focus, 18, 172–214, 263–68
Ford, Gerald, 246
Forsman, Dan, 153
Fox, Arnold, 112
Franco, Carlos, 190

freezing up, 44, 220
frustration, 73–80. *See also* anger
Funk, Fred, 62–63, 66, 177

Gallagher-Smith, Jackie, 189
Gallwey, W. Timothy, 120–21, 230
Garcia, Sergio, 162, 187, 270
Geiberger, Al, 284
Geishauser, Thom, 136, 160
gender, and arousal, 95–96
Gilbert, Larry, 249
Gilder, Bob, 65
Gillespie, Derek, 96–97
Glapski, Jefferson, 75
goals, 112–13
Gogel, Matt, 153
Golbesky, Gary, 30, 184
golf communities, 148–49
"golf rage," 78–80
golf tips, 102–6
golf variations, 163
Goosen, Retief, 7, 65, 144, 255, 285
Goulston, Mark, 255
Graham, Deborah, 208
Graham, Gail, 190, 284–85
Grant, Robert W., 54–55
Green, Sue, 272
Greenberg, Mike, 75
Greene, Don, 256
Greger, Dave, 106
Grieve, Gordon, 88
grinding, 274–79, 285–86
Gropp, Ron, 28
gross motor control, 63, 215–16
Gwang-soo, Choi, 258

Haas, Gene, 23–24
habits, changing, 122
Hackney, Lisa, 212
Hallberg, Gary, 157
Hallowell, Edward M., 40–41, 94, 139, 179
Hanin, Yuri, 51–52
Hannah, Monica, 260
Hanratty, Oliver, 89
Hanson, Tom, 77, 97–98, 227

Harmon, Butch, 176
Hart, Archibald, 165
Harvery, Nancy, 286
Hatalsky, Morris, 216
heart rate, 63
Hemstad, Dave, 155, 244
Henderson, Laura, 185
Hoch, Scott, 64, 98, 258
Hogan, Ben, 64, 68, 98, 143, 195
honesty, 280
hormones, 36–37, 153–54, 232–33, 254–55, 269, 270, 271, 272, 273, 232–35
Hospodar, Michael, 257
humour and golf, 244–47, 272
Hurst, Pat, 65, 95
Hutchinson, Richard, 79–80
hyper flow zone, 89–91

imagery, 193–94
Inkster, Juli, 254, 206, 217, 261
Irwin, Hale, 98, 128, 250, 283–87
Iverson, Becky, 155

Jacobsen, Peter, 25, 164, 178, 192, 246
Jang, Jeong, 239
Janzen, Lee, 66, 138, 194
Jones, Bobby, 64, 76, 144, 164, 282–83, 241, 276; on concentration, 182, 239
Jones, Dale, 77
Jones, Steve, 260
Jordan, Michael, 66–67

Kagan, Jerome, 150
Kaisch, Ken, 77
Kane, Lorie, 6, 65, 138, 206, 282
Keast, Mark, 288
Kerr, Cristie, 276
Kim, Christina, 87
Kim, Mi Hyun, 40
King, Betsy, 157, 213
King, Brad, 209
Kite, Tom, 64, 170
Kupeyan, Calvin, 284

Lacey, Steve, 79
Laffoon, Ky, 77

optimal arousal, 63, 71, 83–91, 154, 225–26, 229
Orlick, Terry, 149, 241
Osborne, Kevin, 78
Osusky, Tony, 79
Otto, Hennie, 74
over-arousal, 67, 84, 94; managing, 226–27, 231–32, 235–49, 258, 259, 262–68; signs of, 78, 228, 230. *See also* stress
oxytocin, 36–37

Pak, Se Ri, 143, 217
Palmer, Arnold, 30, 64, 165, 182, 193, 205, 280; grinding, 286, 285; motivation for, 144, 145
Palmer, Deacon, 145
Palmer, Sandra, 126
Pansing, Tom, 285
Park, Grace, 207, 255–56
Parnevik, Jesper, 138, 190, 245
Pavin, Corey, 64, 251
Payne, Brian, 187
Peck, M. Scott, 73–74, 122
Peete, Calvin, 127
Pelz, Dave, 110, 218–19, 221
pendulum stroke, 216, 218
Penick, Harvey, 147
Peoples, David, 218
Pepper, Dottie, 76–77, 251, 254
Perez, Pat, 66
perfectionists, 178
Persinger, Michael, 259–60
Phillips, Bob, 193
Pitcock, Joan, 227
Player, Gary, 155
pleasure, golfing for, 147–49, 161–68, 201
Plimpton, George, 76
Pooley, Don, 89
Post, Sandra, 230
practice, 106–8, 173–74, 177
preparation, pre-round, 211–12
pre-shot routine, 186–90, 194, 199, 214
pressure, definition of, 44
pressure relievers, 109, 115, 119, 132, 140, 163, 166, 175
Price, Nick, 143, 287

proactive thinking, 127–28
Purdy, Ted, 190
pure pendulum swing, 216, 218
putting, 215–21

Raglin, Jack, 206, 259
recovery, 282–87. *See also* grinding
Reid, Mike, 165
relaxation techniques, 206–9, 238–44, 247–49
religious belief and golf, 155–58
Reynolds, Grey, 261
Rice, Grantland, 113
Rizzo, Patti, 22
Robbins, Kelly, 95
Roberts, Loren, 157
Rodriguez, Chi Chi, 244–45
Roma, Anthony, 269
Rotella, Bob, 68, 97–98, 127–28, 176, 188, 279, 281, 282
routine, pre-shot, 186–90, 194, 199, 214

Sanders, Doug, 64
Saunders, Tom, 138
Saunders, Vivien, 212–13, 283–84
Scherbak, Barbara Bunkowsky, 158
Seheult, Carole, 50–51
self-consciousness, 24–31, 117–19, 149–52
self-esteem, 128, 132
self-evaluation, 30–31, 119, 120–22, 280–82
serotonin, 36–37, 94
Shanley, Andrew, 149
Shapiro, Alan, 113, 114, 120–21, 161, 279–80, 284
Shatz, Mark, 38
Sheehan, Patty, 64
Shepard, Alan, 239
Sheridan, Greg, 256
Shoemaker, Fred, 25, 72, 74, 78, 117, 162, 164, 203
Sieg, Harold, 187–88
Simpson, Scott, 156, 164
Singh, Vijay, 217, 271
small muscles, 215
Smith, Aynsley, 69
Smith, Eugene, 88

ACKNOWLEDGEMENTS

Thank you to those professional and amateur golfers, instructors and psychologists who, over the years, granted me interviews and gave their insights as I was preparing this book, and to the golf organizations that gave me access.

Anyone attempting a book about fear management on the golf course owes a debt to such deep thinkers as Bob Rotella and other sports psychologists and researchers, and to pioneers in the field of moods and emotions, such as Robert Thayer and Daniel Goleman.

Thank you to my wife, Jennifer; our sons, Paul and Kevin; daughter-in-law, Tanya; and granddaughter, Skye; to my parents, Irene and Fred Clarkson; in-laws, Tony and Kathleen Vanderklei and family; and brother Stephen and family, for their support of my meandering career. Thanks as well to the daily newspapers I have worked for, including my present employer, the *Toronto Star*, and sports editors Steve Tustin and Graham Parley; my literary agent, Robert Mackwood of Contemporary Communications; my speaking agents at the National Speakers' Bureau and, at Raincoast, executive Kevin Williams for his enthusiastic support and Derek Fairbridge for his effective editing.

MICHAEL CLARKSON is a journalist who has won numerous awards for his investigative reporting, sports writing and human behavior features. His work has appeared in papers across North America through the *New York Times* and the *Los Angeles Times* syndicates; he now works for the *Toronto Star*. He has also been a contributor to some of the top golf publications, including *Golf Magazine*. His 30-week psychology series on golf.com — the leading golf information source on the internet — was highly acclaimed. Clarkson's first book, *Competitive Fire* (Human Kinetics) was published in 1999. His second book, *Intelligent Fear* (Key Porter) was published in 2001. He lives in Toronto.